Daily Office
Lectionary

REVISED AND UPDATED

A TWO-YEAR BIBLE READING PLAN

ISBN: 9798868157714

reading in both the morning and evening, this revised and updated lectionary is for morning Bible reading.

The primary revision of this lectionary has been the removal of the readings from the Apocryphal or deuterocanonical books. In their place are additional readings from the Old Testament.

While this two-year Bible reading plan will not take you through the entire Bible, it covers the majority of both the Old and New Testaments.

How do I use the Daily Office Lectionary?

A Scripture passage from the Old Testament, the Epistles, and the Gospels are listed for you to read every day.

The readings are organized not around the secular calendar but around the Christian calendar, also called the "Church Year." The readings begin on the First Sunday of Advent which is normally the end of November or beginning of December. We prepare ourselves for the Christmas celebration during the season of Advent marked by the four Sundays before Christmas Day.

Year 1 begins on the First Sunday of Advent preceding *odd-numbered years* that start the next January. Year 2 begins on the First Sunday of Advent preceding *even-numbered years* that start the next January. You can begin this lectionary in Year 1 or Year 2 or at any time during either year!

Year 1 begins during Advent 2022
Year 2 begins during Advent 2023

Year 1 begins during Advent 2024
Year 2 begins during Advent 2025

Year 1 begins during Advent 2026
Year 2 begins during Advent 2027

I came to faith in a Southern Baptist church in the heart of the evangelical tradition. When I was a teenager my Baptist pastors, teachers, and mentors taught me (among other things) to love the Bible. I would spend hours in my teenage bedroom reading the Bible, taking notes, and jotting down my questions. Even after I stepped away from worshiping in a Baptist context, I continued to be devoted to the Scriptures.

As a young pastor in a non-denominational church, I found my Bible reading waning. I struggled with the motivation to read the Bible devotionally when a lot of my work as a pastor included studying, preaching, and teaching the Bible.

Nearly every January I'd pick up a new Bible reading plan. I tried reading a chapter a day. I tried two different versions of *The One-Year Bible*. I tried, and failed to complete, many Bible reading checklists! Nothing seemed to work. I was frustrated.

I felt a bit embarrassed that I could not find my groove. I wanted to be consistent in my Bible reading, but nothing seemed to click until I discovered the Daily Office Lectionary in the back of *The Book of Common Prayer* (BCP), the prayer book of the Episcopal Church. I didn't grow up with a prayer book, but I discovered the BCP when I learned to pray written, liturgical prayers. The lectionary invited me into a simple rhythm of Bible reading that has been life-giving! For years I have used the 1979 BCP during morning prayer which includes Bible reading following the Daily Office Lectionary.

What is a lectionary?
"Lectionary" is a traditional word for a collection of Scripture passages to be read at a particular time. The "daily office" refers to fixed times of prayer throughout the day. While the Church of England designed the Daily Office Lectionary for Scripture

CONTENTS

We continue reading daily after Christmas until Epiphany on January 6. Epiphany marks God's revelation of Jesus to the non-Jewish world. This day remembers the visit of the Magi from the East who came to worship Jesus, the new-born king. Epiphany also recalls the baptism of Jesus and the voice of God the Father who declared Jesus to be his well-beloved Son. The length of the season after the Epiphany varies.

Our readings continue until Ash Wednesday, the beginning of the season of Lent. The day for Ash Wednesday moves from year to year because Lent is the season to prepare for Easter and Easter Sunday moves around. You can locate the date for Ash Wednesday and Easter using the Revised Common Lectionary, a three-year lectionary which provides readings for congregational worship on Sunday mornings. You can access the Revised Common Lectionary online at lectionary.library.vanderbilt.edu.

We continue to read through Eastertide, the season after Easter Sunday until Pentecost Sunday when we remember the outpouring of the Holy Spirit on the Church. After Pentecost we enter Ordinary Time, also known as "The Season after Pentecost." The readings during Ordinary Time are organized around "Propers," so named because they list *the proper* readings for each week. You will determine which Proper to begin with after Pentecost Sunday by the date closest to Pentecost Sunday as noted in italics. The final Sunday in Ordinary Time is "Christ the King Sunday" when we recall that King Jesus is ruling and reigning over all.

The Daily Office Lectionary aligns itself with the sacred calendar that tells the story of Jesus. In doing so, it does not go completely through every book in the Bible before moving on to another Scripture passage. Often this is done because of the changing of the seasons on the Christian calendar.

The best feature of the Daily Office Lectionary is the order of the readings. Every day you will be given a passage from the Old Testament, the Epistles, and the Gospels—in that order. The last thing you will read every day is something *from* Jesus or something *about* Jesus.

What prayers go along with the Daily Office Lectionary?
You will notice that there are no readings from the Psalms in this version of the Daily Office Lectionary. You are encouraged to incorporate the Psalms as prayer, read out loud *as a* prayer, by praying the Psalm for the Day.

You can determine the Psalm for the Day by the Psalm number that coordinates with the day of the secular calendar year. On Day 1 of the year, January 1, pray Psalm 1. On Day 151 start over with Psalm 1 and do the same on day 301.

In addition to praying the Psalm for the Day, prayers are provided at the beginning of each week of Scripture reading passages. These prayers are taken from the 1979 BCP. In the Anglican tradition they are called "Collects" (pronounced CALL-ects). These prayers align themselves with the Christian calendar. You are invited to pray them every day as a part of morning prayer.

My hope is that as you fall into the rhythm of the lectionary and your love for Jesus and the Scriptures grows and flourishes. My prayer for you is a prayer we pray at the end of Ordinary Time.

Blessed Lord, who caused all holy Scriptures to be written for our learning: Grant us so to hear them, read, mark, learn, and inwardly digest them, that we may embrace and ever hold fast the blessed hope of everlasting life, which you have given us in our Savior Jesus Christ; who lives and reigns with you and the Holy Spirit, one God, for ever and ever. Amen.

Derek Vreeland
Christ the King Sunday 2023

YEAR 1

First Sunday of Advent

Almighty God, give us grace to cast away the works of darkness, and put on the armor of light, now in the time of this mortal life in which your Son Jesus Christ came to visit us in great humility; that in the last day, when he shall come again in his glorious majesty to judge both the living and the dead, we may rise to the life immortal; through him who lives and reigns with you and the Holy Spirit, one God, now and for ever. Amen.

Sunday: Isaiah 1:1-9 • 2 Peter 3:1-10 • Matt. 25:1-13

Monday: Isaiah 1:10-20 • 1 Thess. 1:1-10 • Luke 20:1-8

Tuesday: Isaiah 1:21-31 • 1 Thess. 2:1-12 • Luke 20:9-18

Wednesday: Isaiah 2:1-11 • 1 Thess. 2:13-20 • Luke 20:19-26

Thursday: Isaiah 2:12-22 • 1 Thess. 3:1-13 • Luke 20:27-40

Friday: Isaiah 3:8-15 • 1 Thess. 4:1-12 • Luke 20:41-21:4

Saturday: Isaiah 4:2-6 • 1 Thess. 4:13-18 • Luke 21:5-19

Second Sunday of Advent

Merciful God, who sent your messengers the prophets to preach repentance and prepare the way for our salvation: Give us grace to heed their warnings and forsake our sins, that we may greet with joy the coming of Jesus Christ our Redeemer; who lives and reigns with you and the Holy Spirit, one God, now and for ever. Amen.

Sunday: Isaiah 5:1-7 • 2 Peter 3:11-18 • Luke 7:28-35

Monday: Isaiah 5:8-12, 18-23 • 1 Thess. 5:1-11 • Luke 21:20-28

Tuesday: Isaiah 5:13-17, 24-25 • 1 Thess. 5:12-28 • Luke 21:29-38

Wednesday: Isaiah 6:1-13 • 2 Thess. 1:1-12 • John 7:53-8:11

Thursday: Isaiah 7:1-9 • 2 Thess. 2:1-12 • Luke 22:1-13

Friday: Isaiah 7:10-25 • 2 Thess. 2:13-3:5 • Luke 22:14-30

Saturday: Isaiah 8:1-15 • 2 Thess. 3:6-18 • Luke 22:31-38

Third Sunday of Advent
Stir up your power, O Lord, and with great might come among us; and, because we are sorely hindered by our sins, let your bountiful grace and mercy speedily help and deliver us; through Jesus Christ our Lord, to whom, with you and the Holy Spirit, be honor and glory, now and for ever. Amen.

Sunday: Isaiah 13:6-13 • Heb. 12:18-29 • John 3:22-30

Monday: Isaiah 8:16-9:1 • 2 Peter 1:1-11 • Luke 22:39-53

Tuesday: Isaiah 9:1-7 • 2 Peter 1:12-21 • Luke 22:54-69

Wednesday: Isaiah 9:8-17 • 2 Peter 2:1-10a • Mark 1:1-8

Thursday: Isaiah 9:18-10:4 • 2 Peter 2:10b-16 • Matt. 3:1-12

Friday: Isaiah 10:5-19 • 2 Peter 2:17-22 • Matt. 11:2-15

Saturday: Isaiah 10:20-27 • Jude 17-25 • Luke 3:1-9

Fourth Sunday of Advent
Purify our conscience, Almighty God, by your daily visitation, that your Son Jesus Christ, at his coming, may find in us a mansion prepared for himself; who lives and reigns with you, in the unity of the Holy Spirit, one God, now and for ever. Amen.

The readings for this week depend on the date of Christmas Eve. Skip any readings below if they occur before December 24.

Sunday: Isaiah 42:1-12 • Eph. 6:10-20 • John 3:16-21

Monday: Isaiah 11:1-9 • Rev. 20:1-10 • John: 5:30-47

Tuesday: Isaiah 11:10-16 • Rev. 20:11-21:8 • Luke 1:5-25

Wednesday: Isaiah 28:9-22 • Rev. 21:9-21 • Luke 1:26-38

Thursday: Isaiah 29:13-24 • Rev. 21:22-22:5 • Luke 1:39-56

Friday: Isaiah 33:17-22 • Rev. 22:6-11, 18-20 • Luke 1:57-66

Saturday: Isaiah 35:1-10 • Rev. 22:12-17, 21 • Luke 1:67-80

Christmas Eve: Isaiah 59:15b-21 • Phil. 2:5-11

Christmastide

Almighty God, you have poured upon us the new light of your incarnate Word: Grant that this light, enkindled in our hearts, may shine forth in our lives; through Jesus Christ our Lord, who lives and reigns with you, in the unity of the Holy Spirit, one God, now and for ever. Amen.

or

O God, who wonderfully created, and yet more wonderfully restored, the dignity of human nature: Grant that we may share the divine life of him who humbled himself to share our humanity, your Son Jesus Christ; who lives and reigns with you, in the unity of the Holy Spirit, one God, for ever and ever. Amen.

Christmas Day: Zech. 2:10-13 • 1 John 4:7-16 • Matt. 1:18-25

December 26: Isaiah 14:12-23 • Heb. 2:10-18 • John 3:1-15

December 27: Isaiah 14:24-32 • Phil. 2:1-11 • John 3:16-30

December 28: Isaiah 15:1-9 • Phil. 2:1-12-18 • John 3:31-36

December 29: Isaiah 12:1-6 • Rev. 1:1-8 • John 7:37-52

December 30: Isaiah 25:1-9 • Rev. 1:9-20 • John 7:53-8:11

December 31: Isaiah 26:1-9 • 2 Cor. 5:16-6:2 • John 8:12-19

January 1: Gen. 17:1-12a, 15-16 • Col. 2:6-12 • John 16:23b-30

January 2: Gen. 12:1-7 • Heb. 11:1-12 • John 6:35-41, 48-51

January 3: Gen. 28:10-22 • Heb. 11:13-22 • John 10:7-17

January 4: Exodus 3:1-12 • Heb. 11:23-31 • John 14:6-14

January 5: Joshua 1:1-9 • Heb. 11:32-12:2 • John 15:1-16

The Epiphany

O God, by the leading of a star you manifested your only Son to the peoples of the earth: Lead us, who know you now by faith, to your presence, where we may see your glory face to face; through Jesus Christ our Lord, who lives and reigns with you and the Holy Spirit, one God, now and for ever. Amen.

January 6: Isaiah 52:7-10 • Rev. 21:22-27 • Matt. 12:14-21

The readings for the dated days after the Epiphany are used only until the following Saturday before the first Sunday after the Epiphany.

January 7: Isaiah 52:3-6 • Rev. 2:1-7 • John 2:1-11

January 8: Isaiah 59:15-21 • Rev. 2:8-17 • John 4:46-54

January 9: Isaiah 63:1-5 • Rev. 2:18-29 • John 5:1-15

January 10: Isaiah 65:1-9 • Rev. 3:1-6 • John 6:1-14

January 11: Isaiah 65:13-16 • Rev. 3:7-13 • John 6:15-27

January 12: Isaiah 66:1-2, 22-23 • Rev. 3:14-22 • John 9:1-12, 35-38

First Sunday after the Epiphany

Father in heaven, who at the baptism of Jesus in the River Jordan proclaimed him your beloved Son and anointed him with the Holy Spirit: Grant that all who are baptized into his Name may keep the covenant they have made, and boldly confess him as Lord and Savior; who with you and the Holy Spirit lives and reigns, one God, in glory everlasting. Amen.

Sunday: Isaiah 40:1-11 • Heb. 1:1-12 • John 1:1-7, 19-20, 29-34

Monday: Isaiah 40:12-23 • Eph. 1:1-14 • Mark 1:1-13

Tuesday: Isaiah 40:25-31 • Eph. 1:15-23 • Mark 1:14-28

Wednesday: Isaiah 41:1-16 • Eph. 2:1-10 • Mark 1:29-45

Thursday: Isaiah 41:17-29 • Eph. 2:11-22 • Mark 2:1-12

Friday: Isaiah 42:1-17 • Eph. 3:1-13 • Mark 2:13-22

Saturday: Isaiah 43:1-13 • Eph. 3:14-21 • Mark 2:23-3:6

Second Sunday after the Epiphany

Almighty God, whose Son our Savior Jesus Christ is the light of the world: Grant that your people, illumined by your Word and Sacraments, may shine with the radiance of Christ's glory, that he may be known, worshiped, and obeyed to the ends of the earth; through Jesus Christ our Lord, who with you and the Holy Spirit lives and reigns, one God, now and for ever. Amen.

Sunday: Isaiah 43:14-44:5 • Heb. 6:17-7:10 • John 4:27-42

Monday: Isaiah 44:6-8, 21-23 • Eph. 4:1-16 • Mark 3:7-19a

Tuesday: Isaiah 44:9-20 • Eph. 4:17-32 • Mark 3:19b-35

Wednesday: Isaiah 44:24-45:7 • Eph. 5:1-14 • Mark 4:1-20

Thursday: Isaiah 45:5-17 • Eph. 5:15-33 • Mark 4:21-34

Friday: Isaiah 45:18-25 • Eph. 6:1-9 • Mark 4:35-41

Saturday: Isaiah 46:1-13 • Eph. 6:10-24 • Mark 5:1-20

Third Sunday after the Epiphany
Give us grace, O Lord, to answer readily the call of our Savior Jesus Christ and proclaim to all people the Good News of his salvation, that we and the whole world may perceive the glory of his marvelous works; who lives and reigns with you and the Holy Spirit, one God, for ever and ever. Amen.

Sunday: Isaiah 47:1-15 • Heb. 10:19-31 • John 5:2-18

Monday: Isaiah 48:1-11 • Galatians 1:1-17 • Mark 5:21-43

Tuesday: Isaiah 48:12-21 • Galatians 1:18-2:10 • Mark 6:1-13

Wednesday: Isaiah 49:1-12 • Galatians 2:11-21 • Mark 6:13-29

Thursday: Isaiah 49:13-23 • Galatians 3:1-14 • Mark 6:30-46

Friday: Isaiah 50:1-11 • Galatians 3:15-22 • Mark 6:47-56

Saturday: Isaiah 51:1-8 • Galatians 3:23-29 • Mark 7:1-23

Fourth Sunday after the Epiphany

Almighty and everlasting God, you govern all things both in heaven and on earth: Mercifully hear the supplications of your people, and in our time grant us your peace; through Jesus Christ our Lord, who lives and reigns with you and the Holy Spirit, one God, for ever and ever. Amen.

Sunday: Isaiah 51:9-16 • Heb. 11:8-16 • John 7:14-31

Monday: Isaiah 51:17-23 • Galatians 4:1-11 • Mark 7:24-37

Tuesday: Isaiah 52:1-12 • Galatians 4:12-20 • Mark 8:1-10

Wednesday: Isaiah 54:1-17 • Galatians 4:21-31 • Mark 8:11-26

Thursday: Isaiah 55:1-13 • Galatians 5:1-15 • Mark 8:27-9:1

Friday: Isaiah 56:1-8 • Galatians 5:16-24 • Mark 9:2-13

Saturday: Isaiah 57:3-13 • Galatians 5:25-6:10 • Mark 9:14-29

Fifth Sunday after the Epiphany

Set us free, O God, from the bondage of our sins, and give us the liberty of that abundant life which you have made known to us in your Son our Savior Jesus Christ; who lives and reigns with you, in the unity of the Holy Spirit, one God, now and for ever. Amen.

Sunday: Isaiah 57:14-21 • Heb. 12:1-6 • John 7:37-46

Monday: Isaiah 58:1-12 • Galatians 6:11-18 • Mark 9:30-41

Tuesday: Isaiah 59:1-15a • 2 Tim. 1:1-14 • Mark 9:42-50

Wednesday: Isaiah 59:15b-21 • 2 Tim. 1:15-2:13 • Mark 10:1-16

Thursday: Isaiah 60:1-17 • 2 Tim. 2:14-26 • Mark 10:17-31

Friday: Isaiah 61:1-9 • 2 Tim. 3:1-17 • Mark 10:32-45

Saturday: Isaiah 61:10-62:5 • 2 Tim. 4:1-8 • Mark 10:46-52

Sixth Sunday after the Epiphany

O God, the strength of all who put their trust in you: Mercifully accept our prayers; and because in our weakness we can do nothing good without you, give us the help of your grace, that in keeping your commandments we may please you both in will and deed; through Jesus Christ our Lord, who lives and reigns with you and the Holy Spirit, one God, for ever and ever. Amen.

Sunday: Isaiah 62:6-12 • 1 John 2:3-11 • John 8:12-19

Monday: Isaiah 63:1-6 • 1 Tim. 1:1-17 • Mark 11:1-11

Tuesday: Isaiah 63:7-14 • 1 Tim. 1:18-2:8 • Mark 11:12-26

Wednesday: Isaiah 63:15-64:9 • 1 Tim. 3:1-16 • Mark 11:27-12:12

Thursday: Isaiah 65:1-12 • 1 Tim. 4:1-16 • Mark 12:13-27

Friday: Isaiah 65:17-25 • 1 Tim. 5:17-25 • Mark 12:28-34

Saturday: Isaiah 66:1-6 • 1 Tim. 6:6-21 • Mark 12:35-44

Seventh Sunday after the Epiphany

O Lord, you have taught us that without love whatever we do is worth nothing; Send your Holy Spirit and pour into our hearts your greatest gift, which is love, the true bond of peace and of all virtue, without which whoever lives is accounted dead before you. Grant this for the sake of your only Son Jesus Christ, who lives and reigns with you and the Holy Spirit, one God, now and for ever. Amen.

Sunday: Isaiah 66:7-14 • 1 John 3:4-10 • John 10:7-16

Monday: Ruth 1:1-14 • 2 Cor. 1:1-11 • Matt. 5:1-12

Tuesday: Ruth 1:15-22 • 2 Cor. 1:12-22 • Matt. 5:13-20

Wednesday: Ruth 2:1-13 • 2 Cor. 1:23-2:17 • Matt. 5:21-26

Thursday: Ruth 2:14-23 • 2 Cor. 3:1-18 • Matt. 5:27-37

Friday: Ruth 3:1-18 • 2 Cor. 4:1-12 • Matt. 5:38-48

Saturday: Ruth 4:1-17 • 2 Cor. 4:13-5:10 • Matt. 6:1-16

Eighth Sunday after the Epiphany
*Most loving Father, whose will it is for us to give thanks for all things,
to fear nothing but the loss of you, and to cast all our care on you who
care for us: Preserve us from faithless fears and worldly anxieties, that
no clouds of this mortal life may hide from us the light of that love which
is immortal, and which you have manifested to us in your Son Jesus
Christ our Lord; who lives and reigns with you, in the unity of the Holy
Spirit, one God, now and for ever. Amen.*

Sunday: Deut. 4:1-9 • 2 Tim. 4:1-8 • John 12:1-8

Monday: Deut. 4:9-14 • 2 Cor. 10:1-18 • Matt. 6:7-15

Tuesday: Deut. 4:15-24 • 2 Cor. 11:1-21a • Matt. 6:16-23

Wednesday: Deut. 4:23-31 • 2 Cor. 11:21b-33 • Matt. 6:24-34

Thursday: Deut. 4:32-40 • 2 Cor. 12:1-10 • Matt. 7:1-12

Friday: Deut. 5:1-22 • 2 Cor. 12:11-21 • Matt. 7:13-21

Saturday: Deut. 5:22-33 • 2 Cor. 13:1-14 • Matt. 7:22-29

Last Sunday after the Epiphany

O God, who before the passion of your only-begotten Son revealed his glory upon the holy mountain: Grant to us that we, beholding by faith the light of his countenance, may be strengthened to bear our cross, and be changed into his likeness from glory to glory; through Jesus Christ our Lord, who lives and reigns with you and the Holy Spirit, one God, for ever and ever. Amen.

Sunday: Deut. 6:1-9 • Heb. 12:18-29 • John 12:24-32

Monday: Deut. 6:10-15 • Heb. 1:1-14 • John 1:1-18

Tuesday: Deut. 6:16-25 • Heb. 2:1-10 • John 1:19-28

Ash Wednesday

Almighty and everlasting God, you hate nothing you have made and forgive the sins of all who are penitent: Create and make in us new and contrite hearts, that we, worthily lamenting our sins and acknowledging our wretchedness, may obtain of you, the God of all mercy, perfect remission and forgiveness; through Jesus Christ our Lord, who lives and reigns with you and the Holy Spirit, one God, for ever and ever. Amen.

Ash Wednesday: Jonah 3:1-4:11 • Heb. 12:1-14 • Luke 18:9-14

Thursday: Deut. 7:6-11 • Titus 1:1-16 • John 1:29-34

Friday: Deut. 7:12-16 • Titus 2:1-15 • John 1:35-42

Saturday: Deut. 7:17-26 • Titus 3:1-15 • John 1:43-51

First Sunday in Lent

Almighty God, whose blessed Son was led by the Spirit to be tempted by Satan; Come quickly to help us who are assaulted by many temptations; and, as you know the weaknesses of each of us, let each one find you mighty to save; through Jesus Christ your Son our Lord, who lives and reigns with you and the Holy Spirit, one God, now and for ever. Amen.

Sunday: Deut. 8:1-10 • 1 Cor. 1:17-31 • Mark 2:18-22

Monday: Deut. 8:11-20 • Heb. 2:11-18 • John 2:1-12

Tuesday: Deut. 9:4-12 • Heb. 3:1-11 • John 2:13-22

Wednesday: Deut. 9:13-21 • Heb. 3:12-19 • John 2:23-3:15

Thursday: Deut. 9:23-10:5 • Heb. 4:1-10 • John 3:16-21

Friday: Deut. 10:12-22 • Heb. 4:11-16 • John 3:22-36

Saturday: Deut. 11:18-28 • Heb. 5:1-10 • John 4:1-26

Second Sunday in Lent
O God, whose glory it is always to have mercy: Be gracious to all who have gone astray from your ways, and bring them again with penitent hearts and steadfast faith to embrace and hold fast the unchangeable truth of your Word, Jesus Christ your Son; who with you and the Holy Spirit lives and reigns, one God, for ever and ever. Amen.

Sunday: Jer. 1:1-10 • 1 Cor. 3:11-23 • Mark 3:31-4:9

Monday: Jer. 1:11-19 • Rom. 1:1-15 • John 4:27-42

Tuesday: Jer. 2:1-13 • Rom. 1:16-25 • John 4:43-54

Wednesday: Jer. 3:6-18 • Rom. 1:28-2:11 • John 5:1-18

Thursday: Jer. 4:9-10, 19-28 • Rom. 2:12-24 • John 5:19-29

Friday: Jer. 5:1-9 • Rom. 2:25-3:18 • John 5:30-47

Saturday: Jer. 5:20-31 • Rom. 3:19-31 • John 7:1-13

Third Sunday in Lent

Almighty God, you know that we have no power in ourselves to help ourselves: Keep us both outwardly in our bodies and inwardly in our souls, that we may be defended from all adversities which may happen to the body, and from all evil thoughts which may assault and hurt the soul; through Jesus Christ our Lord, who lives and reigns with you and the Holy Spirit, one God, for ever and ever. Amen.

Sunday: Jer. 6:9-15 • 1 Cor. 6:12-20 • Mark 5:1-20

Monday: Jer. 7:1-15 • Rom. 4:1-12 • John 7:14-36

Tuesday: Jer. 7:21-34 • Rom. 4:13-25 • John 7:37-52

Wednesday: Jer. 8:18-9:6 • Rom. 5:1-11 • John 8:12-20

Thursday: Jer. 10:11-24 • Rom. 5:12-21 • John 8:21-32

Friday: Jer. 11:1-8, 14-20 • Rom. 6:1-11 • John 8:33-47

Saturday: Jer. 13:1-11 • Rom. 6:12-23 • John 8:47-59

Fourth Sunday in Lent

Gracious Father, whose blessed Son Jesus Christ came down from heaven to be the true bread which gives life to the world: Evermore give us this bread, that he may live in us, and we in him; who lives and reigns with you and the Holy Spirit, one God, now and for ever. Amen.

Sunday: Jer. 14:1-9, 17-22 • Galatians 4:21-5:1 • Mark 8:11-21

Monday: Jer. 16:10-21 • Rom. 7:1-12 • John 6:1-15

Tuesday: Jer. 17:19-27 • Rom. 7:13-25 • John 6:16-27

Wednesday: Jer. 18:1-11 • Rom. 8:1-11 • John 6:27-40

Thursday: Jer. 22:13-23 • Rom. 8:12-27 • John 6:41-51

Friday: Jer. 23:1-8 • Rom. 8:28-39 • John 6:52-59

Saturday: Jer. 23:9-15 • Rom. 9:1-18 • John 6:60-71

Fifth Sunday in Lent
*Almighty God, you alone can bring into order the unruly wills and
affections of sinners: Grant your people grace to love what you
command and desire what you promise; that, among the swift and
varied changes of the world, our hearts may surely there be fixed where
true joys are to be found; through Jesus Christ our Lord, who lives and
reigns with you and the Holy Spirit, one God, now and for ever. Amen.*

Sunday: Jer. 23:16-32 • 1 Cor. 9:19-27 • Mark 8:31-9:1

Monday: Jer. 24:1-10 • Rom. 9:19-33 • John 9:1-17

Tuesday: Jer. 25:8-17 • Rom. 10:1-13 • John 9:18-41

Wednesday: Jer. 25:30-38 • Rom. 10:14-21 • John 10:1-18

Thursday: Jer. 26:1-16 • Rom. 11:1-12 • John 10:19-42

Friday: Jer. 29:1, 4-13 • Rom. 11:13-24 • John 11:1-27

Saturday: Jer. 31:27-34 • Rom. 11:25-36 • John 11:28-44

Palm Sunday
*Almighty and everliving God, in your tender love for the human race
you sent your Son our Savior Jesus Christ to take upon him our nature,
and to suffer death upon the cross, giving us the example of his great
humility: Mercifully grant that we may walk in the way of his suffering,
and also share in his resurrection; through Jesus Christ our Lord, who*

lives and reigns with you and the Holy Spirit, one God, for ever and ever. Amen.

Palm Sunday: Zech. 9:9-12 • 1 Tim. 6:12-16 • Matt. 21:1-11

Monday: Jer. 12:1-16 • Phil. 3:1-14 • John 12:9-19

Tuesday: Jer. 15:10-21 • Phil. 3:15-21 • John 12:20-26

Wednesday: Jer. 17:5-10, 14-17 • Phil. 4:1-13 • John 12:27-36

Maundy Thursday: Jer. 20:7-11 • 1 Cor. 10:14-17; 11:27-32 • Matthew 26:17-30

Good Friday
Almighty God, we pray you graciously to behold this your family, for whom our Lord Jesus Christ was willing to be betrayed, and given into the hands of sinners, and to suffer death upon the cross; who now lives and reigns with you and the Holy Spirit, one God, for ever and ever. Amen.

Good Friday: Gen. 22:1-14 • 1 Peter 1:10-20 • Matthew 27:32-54

Holy Saturday
O God, Creator of heaven and earth: Grant that, as the crucified body of your dear Son was laid in the tomb and rested on this holy Sabbath, so we may await with him the coming of the third day, and rise with him to newness of life; who now lives and reigns with you and the Holy Spirit, one God, for ever and ever. Amen.

Holy Saturday: Job 19:21-27a • Heb. 4:1-16 • Rom. 8:1-11

Easter Sunday

Almighty God, who through your only-begotten Son Jesus Christ overcame death and opened to us the gate of everlasting life: Grant that we, who celebrate with joy the day of the Lord's resurrection, may be raised from the death of sin by your life-giving Spirit; through Jesus Christ our Lord, who lives and reigns with you and the Holy Spirit, one God, now and for ever. Amen.

Easter Sunday: Exodus 12:1-14 • Phil. 3:7-14 • Luke 24:13-35

Monday: Jonah 2:1-9 • Acts 2:14, 22-32 • John 14:1-14

Tuesday: Isaiah 30:18-21 • Acts 2:36-47 • John 14:15-31

Wednesday: Micah 7:7-15 • Acts 3:1-10 • John 15:1-11

Thursday: Ezekiel 37:1-14 • Acts 3:11-26 • John 15:12-27

Friday: Daniel 12:1-4, 13 • Acts 4:1-12 • John 16:1-15

Saturday: Isaiah 25:1-9 • Acts 4:13-31 • John 16:16-33

Second Sunday of Easter

Almighty and everlasting God, who in the Paschal mystery established the new covenant of reconciliation: Grant that all who have been reborn into the fellowship of Christ's Body may show forth in their lives what they profess by their faith; through Jesus Christ our Lord, who lives and reigns with you and the Holy Spirit, one God, for ever and ever. Amen.

Sunday: Isaiah 43:8-13 • 1 Peter 2:2-10 • John 14:1-7

Monday: Daniel 1:1-21 • 1 John 1:1-10 • John 17:1-11

Tuesday: Daniel 2:1-16 • 1 John 2:1-11 • John 17:12-19

Wednesday: Daniel 2:17-30 • 1 John 2:12-17 • John 17:20-26

Thursday: Daniel 2:31-49 • 1 John 2:18-29 • Luke 3:1-14

Friday: Daniel 3:1-18 • 1 John 3:1-10 • Luke 3:15-22

Saturday: Daniel 3:19-30 • 1 John 3:11-18 • Luke 4:1-13

Third Sunday of Easter
*O God, whose blessed Son made himself known to his disciples in the
breaking of bread: Open the eyes of our faith, that we may behold him in
all his redeeming work; who lives and reigns with you, in the unity of
the Holy Spirit, one God, now and for ever. Amen.*

Sunday: Daniel 4:1-18 • 1 Peter 4:7-11 • John 21:15-25

Monday: Daniel 4:19-27 • 1 John 3:19-4:6 • Luke 4:14-30

Tuesday: Daniel 4:28-37 • 1 John 4:7-21 • Luke 4:31-37

Wednesday: Daniel 5:1-12 • 1 John 5:1-12 • Luke 4:38-44

Thursday: Daniel 5:13-30 • 1 John 5:13-21 • Luke 5:1-11

Friday: Daniel 6:1-15 • 2 John 1-13 • Luke 5:12-26

Saturday: Daniel 6:16-28 • 3 John 1-15 • Luke 5:27-39

Fourth Sunday of Easter
*O God, whose Son Jesus is the good shepherd of your people; Grant that
when we hear his voice we may know him who calls us each by name,
and follow where he leads; who, with you and the Holy Spirit, lives and
reigns, one God, for ever and ever. Amen.*

Sunday: Prov. 13:1-10 • 1 Peter 5:1-11 • Matt. 7:15-29

Monday: Prov. 13:11-25 • Col. 1:1-14 • Luke 6:1-11

Tuesday: Prov. 14:1-19 • Col. 1:15-23 • Luke 6:12-26

Wednesday: Prov. 14:20-35 • Col. 1:24-2:7 • Luke 6:27-38

Thursday: Prov. 15:1-15 • Col. 2:8-23 • Luke 6:39-49

Friday: Prov. 16:1-17 • Col. 3:1-11 • Luke 7:1-17

Saturday: Prov. 16:18-33 • Col. 3:12-17 • Luke 7:18-35

Fifth Sunday of Easter

*Almighty God, whom truly to know is everlasting life: Grant us so
perfectly to know your Son Jesus Christ to be the way, the truth, and the
life, that we may steadfastly follow his steps in the way that leads to
eternal life; through Jesus Christ your Son our Lord, who lives and
reigns with you, in the unity of the Holy Spirit, one God, for ever and
ever. Amen.*

Sunday: Prov. 17:21-28 • 2 Thess. 2:13-17 • Matt. 7:7-14

Monday: Prov. 18:1-11 • Col. 3:18-4:18 • Luke 7:36-50

Tuesday: Prov. 18:12-24 • Rom. 12:1-21 • Luke 8:1-15

Wednesday: Prov. 19:1-17 • Rom. 13:1-14 • Luke 8:16-25

Thursday: Prov. 19:18-29 • Rom. 14:1-12 • Luke 8:26-39

Friday: Prov. 20:15-30 • Rom. 14:13-23 • Luke 8:40-56

Saturday: Prov. 21:1-15 • Rom. 15:1-13 • Luke 9:1-17

Sixth Sunday of Easter

*O God, you have prepared for those who love you such good things as
surpass our understanding: Pour into our hearts such love towards you,
that we, loving you in all things and above all things, may obtain your*

23

promises, which exceed all that we can desire; through Jesus Christ our Lord, who lives and reigns with you and the Holy Spirit, one God, for ever and ever. Amen.

Sunday: Prov. 21:16-29 • 1 Tim. 3:14-4:5 • Matt. 13:24-34a

Monday: Deut. 8:1-10 • James 1:1-15 • Luke 9:18-27

Tuesday: Deut. 8:11-20 • James 1:16-27 • Luke 11:1-13

Wednesday: Prov. 1:1-19 • James 5:13-18 • Luke 12:22-31

Ascension Day: Ezekiel 1:14, 24-28b • Heb. 2:5-18 • Matt. 28:16-20

Friday: Ezekiel 1:28-3:3 • Heb. 4:14-5:6 • Luke 9:28-36

Saturday: Ezekiel 3:4-17 • Heb. 5:7-14 • Luke 9:37-50

Seventh Sunday of Easter
O God, the King of glory, you have exalted your only Son Jesus Christ with great triumph to your kingdom in heaven: Do not leave us comfortless, but send us your Holy Spirit to strengthen us, and exalt us to that place where our Savior Christ has gone before; who lives and reigns with you and the Holy Spirit, one God, in glory everlasting. Amen.

Sunday: Ezekiel 3:16-27 • Eph. 2:1-10 • Matt. 10:24-33, 40-42

Monday: Ezekiel 4:1-17 • Heb. 6:1-12 • Luke 9:51-62

Tuesday: Ezekiel 7:10-15, 23b-27 • Heb. 6:13-20 • Luke 10:1-17

Wednesday: Ezekiel 11:14-25 • Heb. 7:1-17 • Luke 10:17-24

Thursday: Ezekiel 18:1-4, 19-32 • Heb. 7:18-28 • Luke 10:25-37

Friday: Ezekiel 34:17-31 • Heb. 8:1-13 • Luke 10:38-42

Saturday: Ezekiel 43:1-12 • Heb. 9:1-14 • Luke 11:14-23

Pentecost Sunday

Almighty God, on this day you opened the way of eternal life to every race and nation by the promised gift of your Holy Spirit: Shed abroad this gift throughout the world by the preaching of the Gospel, that it may reach to the ends of the earth; through Jesus Christ our Lord, who lives and reigns with you, in the unity of the Holy Spirit, one God, for ever and ever. Amen.

Pentecost Sunday: Isaiah 11:1-9 • 1 Cor. 2:1-13 • John 14:21-29

On the weekdays which follow, the readings are taken from the numbered Proper (one through six) which corresponds most closely to the date of Pentecost.

Ordinary Time

Proper 1
Week of the Sunday closest to May 11

Remember, O Lord, what you have wrought in us and not what we deserve; and, as you have called us to your service, make us worthy of our calling; through Jesus Christ our Lord, who lives and reigns with you and the Holy Spirit, one God, now and for ever. Amen.

Monday: Isaiah 63:7-14 • 2 Tim. 1:1-14 • Luke 11:24-36

Tuesday: Isaiah 63:15-64:9 • 2 Tim. 1:15-2:13 • Luke 11:13-52

Wednesday: Isaiah 65:1-12 • 2 Tim. 2:14-26 • Luke 11:53-12:12

Thursday: Isaiah 65:17-25 • 2 Tim. 3:1-17 • Luke 12:13-31

Friday: Isaiah 66:1-6 • 2 Tim. 4:1-8 • Luke 12:32-48

Saturday: Isaiah 66:7-14 • 2 Tim. 4:9-22 • Luke 12:49-59

Proper 2
Week of the Sunday closest to May 18

Almighty and merciful God, in your goodness keep us, we pray, from all things that may hurt us, that we, being ready both in mind and body, may accomplish with free hearts those things which belong to your purpose; through Jesus Christ our Lord, who lives and reigns with you and the Holy Spirit, one God, now and for ever. Amen.

Monday: Ruth 1:1-18 • 1 Tim. 1:1-17 • Luke 13:1-9

Tuesday: Ruth 1:19-2:13 • 1 Tim. 1:18-2:8 • Luke 13:10-17

Wednesday: Ruth 2:14-23 • 1 Tim. 3:1-16 • Luke 13:18-30

Thursday: Ruth 3:1-18 • 1 Tim. 4:1-16 • Luke 13:31-35

Friday: Ruth 4:1-17 • 1 Tim. 5:17-25 • Luke 14:1-11

Saturday: Deut. 1:1-8 • 1 Tim. 6:6-21 • Luke 14:12-24

Proper 3
Week of the Sunday closest to May 25

Grant, O Lord, that the course of this world may be peaceably governed by your providence; and that your Church may joyfully serve you in confidence and serenity; through Jesus Christ our Lord, who lives and reigns with you and the Holy Spirit, one God, for ever and ever. Amen.

Sunday: Deut. 4:1-9 • Rev. 7:1-4, 9-17 • Matt. 12:33-45

Monday: Deut. 4:9-14 • 2 Cor. 1:1-11 • Luke 14:25-35

Tuesday: Deut. 4:15-24 • 2 Cor. 1:12-22 • Luke 15:1-10

Wednesday: Deut. 4:25-31 • 2 Cor. 1:23-2:17 • Luke 15:1-2, 11-32

Thursday: Deut. 4:32-40 • 2 Cor. 3:1-18 • Luke 16:1-9

Friday: Deut. 5:1-22 • 2 Cor. 4:1-12 • Luke 16:10-18

Saturday: Deut. 5:22-33 • 2 Cor. 4:13-5:10 • Luke 16:19-31

Proper 4
Week of the Sunday closest to June 1

O God, your never-failing providence sets in order all things both in heaven and earth: Put away from us, we entreat you, all hurtful things, and give us those things which are profitable for us; through Jesus Christ our Lord, who lives and reigns with you and the Holy Spirit, one God, for ever and ever. Amen.

Sunday: Deut. 11:1-12 • Rev. 10:1-11 • Matt. 13:44-58

Monday: Deut. 11:13-19 • 2 Cor. 5:11-6:2 • Luke 17:1-10

Tuesday: Deut. 12:1-12 • 2 Cor. 6:3-7:1 • Luke 17:11-19

Wednesday: Deut. 13:1-11 • 2 Cor. 7:2-16 • Luke 17:20-37

Thursday: Deut. 16:18-20; 17:14-20 • 2 Cor. 8:1-16 • Luke 18:1-8

Friday: Deut. 26:1-11 • 2 Cor. 8:16-24 • Luke 18:9-14

Saturday: Deut. 29:2-15 • 2 Cor. 9:1-15 • Luke 18:15-30

Proper 5
Week of the Sunday closest to June 8

O God, from whom all good proceeds: Grant that by your inspiration we may think those things that are right, and by your merciful guiding may do them; through Jesus Christ our Lord, who lives and reigns with you and the Holy Spirit, one God, for ever and ever. Amen.

Sunday: Deut. 29:16-29 • Rev. 12:1-12 • Matt. 15:29-39

Monday: Deut. 30:1-10 • 2 Cor. 10:1-18 • Luke 18:31-43

Tuesday: Deut. 30:11-20 • 2 Cor. 11:1-21a • Luke 19:1-10

Wednesday: Deut. 31:30-32:14 • 2 Cor. 11:21b-33 • Luke 19:11-27

Thursday: Prov. 22:1-16 • 2 Cor. 12:1-10 • Luke 19:28-40

Friday: Prov. 23:1-18 • 2 Cor. 12:11-21 • Luke 19:41-48

Saturday: Prov. 24:3-22 • 2 Cor. 13:1-14 • Luke 20:1-8

Proper 6
Week of the Sunday closest to June 15

Keep, O Lord, your household the Church in your steadfast faith and love, that through your grace we may proclaim your truth with boldness, and minister your justice with compassion; for the sake of our Savior Jesus Christ, who lives and reigns with you and the Holy Spirit, one God, now and for ever. Amen.

Sunday: Prov. 24:23-34 46:11-20 • Rev. 15:1-8 • Matt. 18:1-14

Monday: 1 Sam. 1:1-20 • Acts 1:1-14 • Luke 20:9-19

Tuesday: 1 Sam. 1:21-2:11 • Acts 1:15-26 • Luke 20:19-26

Wednesday: 1 Sam. 2:12-26 • Acts 2:1-21 • Luke 20:27-40

Thursday: 1 Sam. 2:27-36 • Acts 2:22-36 • Luke 20:41-21:4

Friday: 1 Sam. 3:1-21 • Acts 2:37-47 • Luke 21:5-19

Saturday: 1 Sam. 4:1b-11 • Acts 4:32-5:11 • Luke 21:20-28

Proper 7
Week of the Sunday closest to June 22

O Lord, make us have perpetual love and reverence for your holy Name,
for you never fail to help and govern those whom you have set upon the
sure foundation of your loving-kindness; through Jesus Christ our Lord,
who lives and reigns with you and the Holy Spirit, one God, for ever
and ever. Amen.

Sunday: 1 Sam. 4:12-22 • James 1:1-18 • Matt. 19:23-30

Monday: 1 Sam. 5:1-12 • Acts 5:12-26 • Luke 21:29-36

Tuesday: 1 Sam. 6:1-16 • Acts 5:27-42 • Luke 21:37-22:13

Wednesday: 1 Sam. 7:2-17 • Acts 6:1-15 • Luke 22:14-23

Thursday: 1 Sam. 8:1-22 • Acts 6:15-7:16 • Luke 22:24-30

Friday: 1 Sam. 9:1-14 • Acts 7:17-29 • Luke 22:31-38

Saturday: 1 Sam. 9:15-10:1 • Acts 7:30-43 • Luke 22:39-51

Proper 8
Week of the Sunday closest to June 29

Almighty God, you have built your Church upon the foundation of the
apostles and prophets, Jesus Christ himself being the chief cornerstone:

Grant us so to be joined together in unity of spirit by their teaching, that we may be made a holy temple acceptable to you; through Jesus Christ our Lord, who lives and reigns with you and the Holy Spirit, one God, for ever and ever. Amen.

Sunday: 1 Sam. 10:1-16 • Rom. 4:13-25 • Matt. 21:23-32

Monday: 1 Sam. 10:17-27 • Acts 7:44-8:1a • Luke 22:52-62

Tuesday: 1 Sam. 11:1-15 • Acts 8:1-13 • Luke 22:63-71

Wednesday: 1 Sam. 12:1-6, 16-25 • Acts 8:14-25 • Luke 23:1-12

Thursday: 1 Sam. 13:5-18 • Acts 8:26-40 • Luke 23:13-25

Friday: 1 Sam. 13:19-14:15 • Acts 9:1-9 • Luke 23:26-31

Saturday: 1 Sam. 14:16-30 • Acts 9:10-19a • Luke 23:32-43

Proper 9
Week of the Sunday closest to July 6

O God, you have taught us to keep all your commandments by loving you and our neighbor: Grant us the grace of your Holy Spirit, that we may be devoted to you with our whole heart, and united to one another with pure affection; through Jesus Christ our Lord, who lives and reigns with you and the Holy Spirit, one God, for ever and ever. Amen.

Sunday: 1 Sam. 14:36-45 • Rom. 5:1-11 • Matt. 22:1-14

Monday: 1 Sam. 15:1-3, 7-23 • Acts 9:19b-31 • Luke 23:44-56a

Tuesday: 1 Sam. 15:24-35 • Acts 9:32-43 • Luke 23:56b-24:11

Wednesday: 1 Sam. 16:1-13 • Acts 10:1-16 • Luke 24:13-35

Thursday: 1 Sam. 16:14-17:11 • Acts 10:17-33 • Luke 24:36-53

Friday: 1 Sam. 17:17-30 • Acts 10:34-48 • Mark 1:1-13

Saturday: 1 Sam. 17:31-49 • Acts 11:1-18 • Mark 1:14-28

Proper 10
Week of the Sunday closest to July 13

O Lord, mercifully receive the prayers of your people who call upon you, and grant that they may know and understand what things they ought to do, and also may have grace and power faithfully to accomplish them; through Jesus Christ our Lord, who lives and reigns with you and the Holy Spirit, one God, now and for ever. Amen.

Sunday: 1 Sam. 17:50-18:4 • Rom. 10:4-17 • Matt. 23:29-39

Monday: 1 Sam. 18:5-16, 27b-30 • Acts 11:19-30 • Mark 1:29-45

Tuesday: 1 Sam. 19:1-18 • Acts 12:1-17 • Mark 2:1-12

Wednesday: 1 Sam. 20:1-23 • Acts 12:18-25 • Mark 2:13-22

Thursday: 1 Sam. 20:24-42 • Acts 13:1-12 • Mark 2:23-3:6

Friday: 1 Sam. 21:1-15 • Acts 13:13-25 • Mark 3:7-19a

Saturday: 1 Sam. 22:1-23 • Acts 13:26-43 • Mark 3:19b-35

Proper 11
Week of the Sunday closest to July 20

Almighty God, the fountain of all wisdom, you know our necessities before we ask and our ignorance in asking: Have compassion on our weakness, and mercifully give us those things which for our unworthiness we dare not, and for our blindness we cannot ask; through the worthiness of your Son Jesus Christ our Lord, who lives and reigns with you and the Holy Spirit, one God, now and for ever. Amen.

Sunday: 1 Sam. 23:7-18 • Rom. 11:33-12:2 • Matt. 25:14-30

Monday: 1 Sam. 24:1-22 • Acts 13:44-52 • Mark 4:1-20

Tuesday: 1 Sam. 25:1-22 • Acts 14:1-18 • Mark 4:21-34

Wednesday: 1 Sam. 25:23-44 • Acts 14:19-28 • Mark 4:35-41

Thursday: 1 Sam. 28:3-20 • Acts 15:1-11 • Mark 5:1-20

Friday: 1 Sam. 31:1-13 • Acts 15:12-21 • Mark 5:21-43

Saturday: 2 Sam. 1:1-16 • Acts 15:22-35 • Mark 6:1-13

Proper 12
Week of the Sunday closest to July 27

O God, the protector of all who trust in you, without whom nothing is strong, nothing is holy: Increase and multiply upon us your mercy; that, with you as our ruler and guide, we may so pass through things temporal, that we lose not the things eternal; through Jesus Christ our Lord, who lives and reigns with you and the Holy Spirit, one God, for ever and ever. Amen.

Sunday: 2 Sam. 1:17-27 • Rom. 12:9-21 • Matt. 25:31-46

Monday: 2 Sam. 2:1-11 • Acts 15:36-16:5 • Mark 6:14-29

Tuesday: 2 Sam. 3:6-21 • Acts 16:6-15 • Mark 6:30-46

Wednesday: 2 Sam. 3:22-39 • Acts 16:16-24 • Mark 6:47-56

Thursday: 2 Sam. 4:1-12 • Acts 16:25-40 • Mark 7:1-23

Friday: 2 Sam. 5:1-12 • Acts 17:1-15 • Mark 7:24-37

Saturday: 2 Sam. 5:22-6:11 • Acts 17:16-34 • Mark 8:1-10

Proper 13
Week of the Sunday closest to August 3

Let your continual mercy, O Lord, cleanse and defend your Church; and, because it cannot continue in safety without your help, protect and govern it always by your goodness; through Jesus Christ our Lord, who lives and reigns with you and the Holy Spirit, one God, for ever and ever. Amen.

Sunday: 2 Sam. 6:12-23 • Rom. 14:7-12 • John 1:43-51

Monday: 2 Sam. 7:1-17 • Acts 18:1-11 • Mark 8:11-21

Tuesday: 2 Sam. 7:18-29 • Acts 18:12-28 • Mark 8:22-33

Wednesday: 2 Sam. 9:1-13 • Acts 19:1-10 • Mark 8:34-9:1

Thursday: 2 Sam. 11:1-27 • Acts 19:11-20 • Mark 9:2-13

Friday: 2 Sam. 12:1-14 • Acts 19:21-41 • Mark 9:14-29

Saturday: 2 Sam. 12:15-31 • Acts 20:1-16 • Mark 9:30-41

Proper 14
Week of the Sunday closest to August 10

Grant to us, Lord, we pray, the spirit to think and do always those things that are right, that we, who cannot exist without you, may by you be enabled to live according to your will; through Jesus Christ our Lord, who lives and reigns with you and the Holy Spirit, one God, for ever and ever. Amen.

Sunday: 2 Sam. 13:1-22 • Rom. 15:1-13 • John 3:22-36

Monday: 2 Sam. 13:23-39 • Acts 20:17-38 • Mark 9:42-50

Tuesday: 2 Sam. 14:1-20 • Acts 21:1-14 • Mark 10:1-16

Wednesday: 2 Sam. 14:21-33 • Acts 21:15-26 • Mark 10:17-31

Thursday: 2 Sam. 15:1-18 • Acts 21:27-36 • Mark 10:32-45

Friday: 2 Sam. 15:19-37 • Acts 21:37-22:16 • Mark 10:46-52

Saturday: 2 Sam. 16:1-23 • Acts 22:17-29 • Mark 11:1-11

Proper 15
Week of the Sunday closest to August 17

Almighty God, you have given your only Son to be for us a sacrifice for sin, and also an example of godly life: Give us grace to receive thankfully the fruits of this redeeming work, and to follow daily in the blessed steps of his most holy life; through Jesus Christ your Son our Lord, who lives and reigns with you and the Holy Spirit, one God, now and for ever. Amen.

Sunday: 2 Sam. 17:1-23 • Galatians 3:6-14 • John 5:30-47

Monday: 2 Sam. 17:24-18:8 • Acts 22:30-23:11 • Mark 11:12-26

Tuesday: 2 Sam. 18:9-18 • Acts 23:12-24 • Mark 11:27-12:12

Wednesday: 2 Sam. 18:19-33 • Acts 23:23-35 • Mark 12:13-27

Thursday: 2 Sam. 19:1-23 • Acts 24:1-23 • Mark 12:28-34

Friday: 2 Sam. 19:24-43 • Acts 24:24-25:12 • Mark 12:35-44

Saturday: 2 Sam. 23:1-7, 13-17 • Acts 25:13-27 • Mark 13:1-13

Proper 16

Week of the Sunday closest to August 24

Grant, O merciful God, that your Church, being gathered together in unity by your Holy Spirit, may show forth your power among all peoples, to the glory of your Name; through Jesus Christ our Lord, who lives and reigns with you and the Holy Spirit, one God, for ever and ever. Amen.

Sunday: 2 Sam. 24:1-2, 10-25 • Galatians 3:23-4:7 • John 8:12-20

Monday: 1 Kings 1:5-31 • Acts 26:1-23 • Mark 13:14-27

Tuesday: 1 Kings 1:38-2:4 • Acts 26:24-27:8 • Mark 13:28-37

Wednesday: 1 Kings 3:1-15 • Acts 27:9-26 • Mark 14:1-11

Thursday: 1 Kings 3:16-28 • Acts 27:27-44 • Mark 14:12-26

Friday: 1 Kings 5:1-6:1, 7 • Acts 28:1-16 • Mark 14:27-42

Saturday: 1 Kings 7:51-8:21 • Acts 28:17-31 • Mark 14:43-52

Proper 17

Week of the Sunday closest to August 31

Lord of all power and might, the author and giver of all good things: Graft in our hearts the love of your Name; increase in us true religion; nourish us with all goodness; and bring forth in us the fruit of good works; through Jesus Christ our Lord, who lives and reigns with you and the Holy Spirit, one God, for ever and ever. Amen.

Sunday: 1 Kings 8:22-40 • 1 Tim. 4:7b-16 • John 8:47-59

Monday: 2 Chronicles 6:32-7:7 • James 2:1-13 • Mark 14:53-65

Tuesday: 1 Kings 8:65-9:9 • James 2:14-26 • Mark 14:66-72

Wednesday: 1 Kings 9:24-10:13 • James 3:1-12 • Mark 15:1-11

Thursday: 1 Kings 11:1-13 • James 3:13-4:12 • Mark 15:12-21

Friday: 1 Kings 11:26-43 • James 4:13-5:6 • Mark 15:22-32

Saturday: 1 Kings 12:1-20 • James 5:7-12, 19-20 • Mark 15:33-39

Proper 18
Week of the Sunday closest to September 7

Grant us, O Lord, to trust in you with all our hearts; for, as you always resist the proud who confide in their own strength, so you never forsake those who make their boast of your mercy; through Jesus Christ our Lord, who lives and reigns with you and the Holy Spirit, one God, now and for ever. Amen.

Sunday: 1 Kings 12:21-33 • Acts 4:18-31 • John 10:31-42

Monday: 1 Kings 13:1-10 • Phil. 1:1-11 • Mark 15:40-47

Tuesday: 1 Kings 16:23-34 • Phil. 1:12-30 • Mark 16:1-20

Wednesday: 1 Kings 17:1-24 • Phil. 2:1-11 • Matt. 2:1-12

Thursday: 1 Kings 18:1-19 • Phil. 2:12-30 • Matt. 2:13-23

Friday: 1 Kings 18:20-40 • Phil. 3:1-16 • Matt. 3:1-12

Saturday: 1 Kings 18:41-19:8 • Phil. 3:17-4:7 • Matt. 3:13-17

Proper 19
Week of the Sunday closest to September 14

O God, because without you we are not able to please you, mercifully grant that your Holy Spirit may in all things direct and rule our hearts; through Jesus Christ our Lord, who lives and reigns with you and the Holy Spirit, one God, now and for ever. Amen.

Sunday: 1 Kings 19:8-21 • Acts 5:34-42 • John 11:45-57

Monday: 1 Kings 21:1-16 • 1 Cor. 1:1-19 • Matt. 4:1-11

Tuesday: 1 Kings 21:17-29 • 1 Cor. 1:20-31 • Matt. 4:12-17

Wednesday: 1 Kings 22:1-28 • 1 Cor. 2:1-13 • Matt. 4:18-25

Thursday: 1 Kings 22:29-45 • 1 Cor. 2:14-3:15 • Matt. 5:1-10

Friday: 2 Kings 1:2-17 • 1 Cor. 3:16-23 • Matt. 5:11-16

Saturday: 2 Kings 2:1-18 • 1 Cor. 4:1-7 • Matt. 5:17-20

Proper 20
Week of the Sunday closest to September 21

Grant us, Lord, not to be anxious about earthly things, but to love things heavenly; and even now, while we are placed among things that are passing away, to hold fast to those that shall endure; through Jesus Christ our Lord, who lives and reigns with you and the Holy Spirit, one God, for ever and ever. Amen.

Sunday: 2 Kings 4:8-37 • Acts 9:10-31 • Luke 3:7-18

Monday: 2 Kings 5:1-19 • 1 Cor. 4:8-21 • Matt. 5:21-26

Tuesday: 2 Kings 5:19-27 • 1 Cor. 5:1-8 • Matt. 5:27-37

Wednesday: 2 Kings 6:1-23 • 1 Cor. 5:9-6:8 • Matt. 5:38-48

Thursday: 2 Kings 9:1-16 • 1 Cor. 6:12-20 • Matt. 6:1-6, 16-18

Friday: 2 Kings 9:17-37 • 1 Cor. 7:1-9 • Matt. 6:7-15

Saturday: 2 Kings 11:1-20a • 1 Cor. 7:10-24 • Matt. 6:19-24

Proper 21
Week of the Sunday closest to September 28

*O God, you declare your almighty power chiefly in showing mercy and
pity: Grant us the fullness of your grace, that we, running to obtain
your promises, may become partakers of your heavenly treasure;
through Jesus Christ our Lord, who lives and reigns with you and the
Holy Spirit, one God, for ever and ever. Amen.*

Sunday: 2 Kings 17:1-18 • Acts 9:36-43 • Luke 5:1-11

Monday: 2 Kings 17:24-41 • 1 Cor. 7:25-31 • Matt. 6:25-34

Tuesday: 2 Chronicles 29:1-3; 30:1-27 • 1 Cor. 7:32-40 • Matt.
7:1-12

Wednesday: 2 Kings 18:9-25 • 1 Cor. 8:1-13 • Matt. 7:13-21

Thursday: 2 Kings 18:28-37 • 1 Cor. 9:1-15 • Matt. 7:22-29
Friday: 2 Kings 19:1-20 • 1 Cor. 9:16-27 • Matt. 8:1-17

Saturday: 2 Kings 19:21-36 • 1 Cor. 10:1-13 • Matt. 8:18-27

Proper 22
Week of the Sunday closest to October 5

*Almighty and everlasting God, you are always more ready to hear than
we to pray, and to give more than we either desire or deserve: Pour upon*

us the abundance of your mercy, forgiving us those things of which our conscience is afraid, and giving us those good things for which we are not worthy to ask, except through the merits and mediation of Jesus Christ our Savior; who lives and reigns with you and the Holy Spirit, one God, for ever and ever. Amen.

Sunday: 2 Kings 20:1-21 • Acts 12:1-17 • Luke 7:11-17

Monday: 2 Kings 21:1-18 • 1 Cor. 10:14-11:1 • Matt. 8:28-34

Tuesday: 2 Kings 22:1-13 • 1 Cor. 11:2, 17-22 • Matt. 9:1-8

Wednesday: 2 Kings 22:14-23:3 • 1 Cor 11:23-34 • Matt. 9:9-17

Thursday: 2 Kings 23:4-25 • 1 Cor. 12:1-11 • Matt. 9:18-26

Friday: 2 Kings 23:36-24:17 • 1 Cor. 12:12-26 • Matt. 9:27-34

Saturday: Jer. 35:1-19 • 1 Cor. 12:27-13:3 • Matt. 9:35-10:4

Proper 23
Week of the Sunday closest to October 12

Lord, we pray that your grace may always precede and follow us, that we may continually be given to good works; through Jesus Christ our Lord, who lives and reigns with you and the Holy Spirit, one God, now and for ever. Amen.

Sunday: Jer. 36:1-10 • Acts 14:8-18 • Luke 7:36-50

Monday: Jer. 36:11-26 • 1 Cor. 13:1-13 • Matt. 10:5-15

Tuesday: Jer. 36:27-37:2 • 1 Cor. 14:1-12 • Matt. 10:16-23

Wednesday: Jer. 37:3-21 • 1 Cor. 14:13-25 • Matt. 10:24-33

Thursday: Jer. 38:1-13 • 1 Cor. 14:26-33a, 37-40 • Matt. 10:34-42

Friday: Jer. 38:14-28 • 1 Cor. 15:1-11 • Matt. 11:1-6

Saturday: 2 Kings 25:8-26 • 1 Cor. 15:12-29 • Matt. 11:7-15

Proper 24
Week of the Sunday closest to October 19

*Almighty and everlasting God, in Christ you have revealed your glory
among the nations: Preserve the works of your mercy, that your Church
throughout the world may persevere with steadfast faith in the
confession of your Name; through Jesus Christ our Lord, who lives and
reigns with you and the Holy Spirit, one God, for ever and ever. Amen.*

Sunday: Jer. 29:1, 4-14 • Acts 16:6-15 • Luke 10:1-12, 17-20

Monday: Jer. 44:1-14 • 1 Cor. 15:30-41 • Matt. 11:16-24

Tuesday: Lam. 1:1-12 • 1 Cor. 15:41-50 • Matt. 11:25-30

Wednesday: Lam. 2:8-15 • 1 Cor. 15:51-58 • Matt. 12:1-14

Thursday: Ezra 1:1-11 • 1 Cor. 16:1-9 • Matt. 12:15-21

Friday: Ezra 3:1-13 • 1 Cor. 16:10-24 • Matt. 12:22-32

Saturday: Ezra 4:7, 11-24 • Philemon 1-24 • Matt. 12:33-42

Proper 25
Week of the Sunday closest to October 26

*Almighty and everlasting God, increase in us the gifts of faith, hope,
and charity; and, that we may obtain what you promise, make us love
what you command; through Jesus Christ our Lord, who lives and
reigns with you and the Holy Spirit, one God, for ever and ever. Amen.*

Sunday: Haggai 1:1-2:9 • Acts 18:24-19:7 • Luke 10:25-37

Monday: Zech. 1:7-17 • Rev. 1:4-20 • Matt. 12:43-50

Tuesday: Ezra 5:1-17 • Rev. 4:1-11 • Matt. 13:1-9

Wednesday: Ezra 6:1-22 • Rev. 5:1-10 • Matt. 13:10-17

Thursday: Nehemiah 1:1-11 • Rev. 5:11-6:11 • Matt. 13:18-23

Friday: Nehemiah 2:1-20 • Rev. 6:12-7:4 • Matt. 13:24-30

Saturday: Nehemiah 4:1-23 • Rev. 7:4-17 • Matt. 13:31-55

Proper 26
Week of the Sunday closest to November 2

*Almighty and merciful God, it is only by your gift that your faithful
people offer you true and laudable service: Grant that we may run
without stumbling to obtain your heavenly promises; through Jesus
Christ our Lord, who lives and reigns with you and the Holy Spirit, one
God, now and for ever. Amen.*

Sunday: Nehemiah 5:1-19 • Acts 20:7-12 • Luke 12:22-31

Monday: Nehemiah 6:1-19 • Rev. 10:1-11 • Matt. 13:36-43

Tuesday: Nehemiah 12:27-31a, 42b-47 • Rev. 11:1-19 • Matt.
13:44-52

Wednesday: Nehemiah 13:4-22 • Rev. 12:1-12 • Matt. 13:53-58

Thursday: Ezra 7:1-26 • Rev. 14:1-13 • Matt. 14:1-12

Friday: Ezra 7:27-28; 8:21-36 • Rev. 15:1-8 • Matt. 14:13-21

Saturday: Ezra 9:1-15 • Rev. 17:1-14 • Matt. 14:22-36

Proper 27

Week of the Sunday closest to November 9

O God, whose blessed Son came into the world that he might destroy the works of the devil and make us children of God and heirs of eternal life: Grant that, having this hope, we may purify ourselves as he is pure; that, when he comes again with power and great glory, we may be made like him in his eternal and glorious kingdom; where he lives and reigns with you and the Holy Spirit, one God, for ever and ever. Amen.

Sunday: Ezra 10:1-17 • Acts 24:10-21 • Luke 14:12-24

Monday: Nehemiah 9:1-25 • Rev. 18:1-8 • Matt. 15:1-20

Tuesday: Nehemiah 9:26-38 • Rev. 18:9-20 • Matt. 15:21-28

Wednesday: Nehemiah 7:73b-8:3, 5-18 • Rev. 18:21-24 • Matt. 15:29-39

Thursday: Prov. 2:10-22 • Rev. 19:1-10 • Matt. 16:1-12

Friday: Prov. 3:1-10 • Rev. 19:11-16 • Matt. 16:13-20

Saturday: Prov. 6:20-35 • Rev. 20:1-6 • Matt. 16:21-28

Proper 28

Week of the Sunday closest to November 16

Blessed Lord, who caused all holy Scriptures to be written for our learning: Grant us so to hear them, read, mark, learn, and inwardly digest them, that we may embrace and ever hold fast the blessed hope of everlasting life, which you have given us in our Savior Jesus Christ; who lives and reigns with you and the Holy Spirit, one God, for ever and ever. Amen.

Sunday: Prov. 10:13-22 • Acts 28:14b-23 • Luke 16:1-13

Monday: Prov. 10:23-32 • Rev. 20:7-15 • Matt. 17:1-13

Tuesday: Prov. 11:1-16 • Rev. 21:1-8 • Matt. 17:14-21

Wednesday: Prov. 11:17-31 • Rev. 21:9-21 • Matt. 17:22-27

Thursday: Prov. 12:1-16 • Rev. 21:22-22:5 • Matt. 18:1-9

Friday: Prov. 12:17-28 • Rev. 22:6-13 • Matt. 18:10-20

Saturday: Isaiah 65:17-25 • Rev. 22:14-21 • Matt. 18:21-35

Proper 29
Week of the Sunday closest to November 23

Almighty and everlasting God, whose will it is to restore all things in your well-beloved Son, the King of kings and Lord of lords: Mercifully grant that the peoples of the earth, divided and enslaved by sin, may be freed and brought together under his most gracious rule; who lives and reigns with you and the Holy Spirit, one God, now and for ever. Amen.

Christ the King Sunday: Isaiah 19:19-25 • Rom. 15:5-13 • Luke 19:11-27

Monday: Joel 3:1-2, 9-17 • 1 Peter 1:1-12 • Matt. 19:1-12

Tuesday: Nahum 1:1-13 • 1 Peter 1:13-25 • Matt. 19:13-22

Wednesday: Obadiah 15-21 • 1 Peter 2:1-10 • Matt. 19:23-30

Thursday: Zephaniah 3:1-13 • 1 Peter 2:11-25 • Matt. 20:1-16

Friday: Isaiah 24:14-23 • 1 Peter 3:13-4:6 • Matt. 20:17-28

Saturday: Micah 7:11-20 • 1 Peter 4:7-19 • Matt. 20:29-34

Year 2

First Sunday of Advent

Almighty God, give us grace to cast away the works of darkness, and put on the armor of light, now in the time of this mortal life in which your Son Jesus Christ came to visit us in great humility; that in the last day, when he shall come again in his glorious majesty to judge both the living and the dead, we may rise to the life immortal; through him who lives and reigns with you and the Holy Spirit, one God, now and for ever. Amen.

Sunday: Amos 1:1-5, 13-2:8 • 1 Thess. 5:1-11 • Luke 21:5-19

Monday: Amos 2:6-16 • 2 Peter 1:1-11 • Matt. 21:1-11

Tuesday: Amos 3:1-11 • 2 Peter 1:12-21 • Matt. 21:12-22

Wednesday: Amos 3:12-4:5 • 2 Peter 3:1-10 • Matt. 21:23-32

Thursday: Amos 4:6-13 • 2 Peter 3:11-18 • Matt. 21:33-46

Friday: Amos 5:1-17 • Jude 1-16 • Matt. 22:1-14

Saturday: Amos 5:18-27 • Jude 17-25 • Matt. 22:15-22

Second Sunday of Advent

Merciful God, who sent your messengers the prophets to preach repentance and prepare the way for our salvation: Give us grace to heed their warnings and forsake our sins, that we may greet with joy the coming of Jesus Christ our Redeemer; who lives and reigns with you and the Holy Spirit, one God, now and for ever. Amen.

Sunday: Amos 6:1-14 • 2 Thess. 1:5-12 • Luke 1:57-67

Monday: Amos 7:1-9 • Rev. 1:1-8 • Matt. 22:23-33

Tuesday: Amos 7:10-17 • Rev. 1:9-16 • Matt. 22:34-46

Wednesday: Amos 8:1-14 • Rev. 1:17-2:7 • Matt. 23:1-12

Thursday: Amos 9:1-10 • Rev. 2:8-17 • Matt. 23:13-26

Friday: Haggai 1:1-15 • Rev. 2:18-29 • Matt. 23:27-39

Saturday: Haggai 2:1-9 • Rev. 3:1-6 • Matt. 24:1-14

Third Sunday of Advent
Stir up your power, O Lord, and with great might come among us; and, because we are sorely hindered by our sins, let your bountiful grace and mercy speedily help and deliver us; through Jesus Christ our Lord, to whom, with you and the Holy Spirit, be honor and glory, now and for ever. Amen.

Sunday: Amos 9:11-15 • 2 Thess. 2:1-3, 13-17 • John 5:30-47

Monday: Zech. 1:7-17 • Rev. 3:7-13 • Matt. 24:15-31

Tuesday: Zech. 2:1-13 • Rev. 3:14-22 • Matt. 24:32-44

Wednesday: Zech. 3:1-10 • Rev. 4:1-8 • Matt. 24:45-51

Thursday: Zech. 4:1-14 • Rev. 4:9-5:5 • Matt. 25:1-13

Friday: Zech. 7:8-8:8 • Rev. 5:6-14 • Matt. 25:14-30

Saturday: Zech. 8:9-17 • Rev. 6:1-17 • Matt. 25:31-46

Fourth Sunday of Advent
Purify our conscience, Almighty God, by your daily visitation, that your Son Jesus Christ, at his coming, may find in us a mansion prepared for himself; who lives and reigns with you, in the unity of the Holy Spirit, one God, now and for ever. Amen.

The readings for this week depend on the date of Christmas Eve. Skip any readings below if they occur before December 24.

Sunday: Gen. 3:8-15 • Rev. 12:1-10 • John 3:16-21

Monday: Zephaniah 3:14-20 • Titus 1:1-16 • Luke 1:1-25

Tuesday: 1 Sam. 2:1b-10 • Titus 2:1-10 • Luke 1:26-38

Wednesday: 2 Sam. 7:1-17 • Titus 2:11-3:8a • Luke 1:39-56

Thursday: 2 Sam. 7:18-29 • Galatians 3:1-14 • Luke 1:57-66

Friday: Isaiah 2:1-11 • Galatians 3:15-22 • Luke 1:67-80

Saturday: Isaiah 59:15b-21 • Phil. 2:5-11 • Matt. 1:1-17

Christmas Eve: Isaiah 9:1-7 • Galatians 3:23-4:7 • Matt. 1:18-25

Christmastide

Almighty God, you have poured upon us the new light of your incarnate Word: Grant that this light, enkindled in our hearts, may shine forth in our lives; through Jesus Christ our Lord, who lives and reigns with you, in the unity of the Holy Spirit, one God, now and for ever. Amen.

or

O God, who wonderfully created, and yet more wonderfully restored, the dignity of human nature: Grant that we may share the divine life of him who humbled himself to share our humanity, your Son Jesus Christ; who lives and reigns with you, in the unity of the Holy Spirit, one God, for ever and ever. Amen.

Christmas Day: Micah 4:1-5; 5:2-4 • 1 John 4:7-16 • Luke 2:1-14

December 26: Isaiah 5:1-7 • Luke 2:15-21 • Colossians 1:3-14

December 27: Isaiah 11:1-9 • Luke 2:22-40 •Colossians 1:15-23

December 28: 1 Sam. 1:1-2, 7b-28 • Col. 1:9-20 • Luke 24:1-52

December 29: 2 Sam. 23:13-17b • 2 John -13 • John 2:1-11

December 30: 1 Kings 17:17-24 • 3 John 1-14 • John 4:46-54

December 31: 1 Kings 3:5-14 • James 4:13-17; 5:7-11 • John 5:1-15

January 1: Isaiah 62:1-5, 10-12 • Rev. 19:11-16 • Matt. 1:18-25

January 2: 1 Kings 19:1-8 • Eph. 4:1-16 • John 6:1-14

January 3: 1 Kings 19:9-18 • Eph. 4:17-32 • John 6:15-27

January 4: Joshua 3:14-4:7 • Eph. 5:1-20 • John 9:1-12, 35-38

January 5: Jonah 2:2-9 • Eph. 6:10-20 • John 11:17-27, 38-44

The Epiphany
O God, by the leading of a star you manifested your only Son to the peoples of the earth: Lead us, who know you now by faith, to your presence, where we may see your glory face to face; through Jesus Christ our Lord, who lives and reigns with you and the Holy Spirit, one God, now and for ever. Amen.

January 6: Isaiah 49:1-7 • Rev. 21:22-27 • Matt. 12-14-21

The readings for the dated days after the Epiphany are used only until the following Saturday before the first Sunday after the Epiphany.

January 7: Deut. 8:1-3 • Col. 1:1-14 • John 6:30-33, 48-51

January 8: Exodus 17:1-7 • Col. 1:15-23 • John 7:37-52

January 9: Isaiah 45:14-19 • Col. 1:21-2:7 • John 8:12-19

January 10: Jer. 23:1-8 • Col. 2:8-23 • John 10:7-17

January 11: Isaiah 55:3-9 • Col. 3:1-17 • John 14:6-14

January 12: Gen. 49:1-2, 8-12 • Col. 3:18-4:6 • John 15:1-16

First Sunday after the Epiphany
Father in heaven, who at the baptism of Jesus in the River Jordan proclaimed him your beloved Son and anointed him with the Holy Spirit: Grant that all who are baptized into his Name may keep the covenant they have made, and boldly confess him as Lord and Savior; who with you and the Holy Spirit lives and reigns, one God, in glory everlasting. Amen.

Sunday: Gen. 1:1-2:3 • Eph. 1:3-14 • John 1:29-34

Monday: Gen. 2:4-25 • Heb. 1:1-14 • John 1:1-18

Tuesday: Gen. 3:1-24 • Heb. 2:1-10 • John 1:19-28

Wednesday: Gen. 4:1-16 • Heb. 2:11-18 • John 1:29-42

Thursday: Gen. 4:17-26 • Heb. 3:1-11 • John 1:43-51

Friday: Gen. 6:1-8 • Heb. 3:12-19 • John 2:1-12

Saturday: Gen. 6:9-22 • Heb. 4:1-13 • John 2:13-22

Second Sunday after the Epiphany
Almighty God, whose Son our Savior Jesus Christ is the light of the world: Grant that your people, illumined by your Word and Sacraments, may shine with the radiance of Christ's glory, that he may be known, worshiped, and obeyed to the ends of the earth; through Jesus Christ our Lord, who with you and the Holy Spirit lives and reigns, one God, now and for ever. Amen.

Sunday: Gen. 7:1-10, 17-23 • Eph. 4:1-16 • Mark 3:7-19

Monday: Gen. 8:6-22 • Heb. 4:14-5:6 • John 2:23-3:15

Tuesday: Gen. 9:1-17 • Heb. 5:7-14 • John 3:16-21

Wednesday: Gen. 9:18-29 • Heb. 6:1-12 • John 3:22-36

Thursday: Gen. 11:1-9 • Heb. 6:13-20 • John 4:1-15

Friday: Gen. 11:27-12:8 • Heb. 7:1-17 • John 4:16-26

Saturday: Gen. 12:9-13:1 • Heb. 7:18-28 • John 4:27-42

Third Sunday after the Epiphany
Give us grace, O Lord, to answer readily the call of our Savior Jesus Christ and proclaim to all people the Good News of his salvation, that we and the whole world may perceive the glory of his marvelous works; who lives and reigns with you and the Holy Spirit, one God, for ever and ever. Amen.

Sunday: Gen. 13:2-138 • Galatians 2:1-10 • Mark 7:31-37

Monday: Gen. 14:1-24 • Heb. 8:1-13 • John 4:43-54

Tuesday: Gen. 15:1-11, 17-21 • Heb. 9:1-14 • John 5:1-18

Wednesday: Gen. 16:1-14 • Heb. 9:15-28 • John 5:19-29

Thursday: Gen. 16:15-17:14 • Heb. 10:1-10 • John 5:30-47

Friday: Gen. 17:15-27 • Heb. 10:11-25 • John 6:1-15

Saturday: Gen. 18:1-16 • Heb. 10:26-39 • John 6:16-27

Fourth Sunday after the Epiphany

Almighty and everlasting God, you govern all things both in heaven and on earth: Mercifully hear the supplications of your people, and in our time grant us your peace; through Jesus Christ our Lord, who lives and reigns with you and the Holy Spirit, one God, for ever and ever. Amen.

Sunday: Gen. 18:16-33 • Galatians 5:13-25 • Mark 8:22-30

Monday: Gen. 19:1-17, 24-29 • Heb. 11:1-12 • John 6:27-40

Tuesday: Gen. 21:1-21 • Heb. 11:13-22 • John 6:41-51

Wednesday: Gen. 22:1-18 • Heb. 11:23-31 • John 6:52-59

Thursday: Gen. 23:1-20 • Heb. 11:32-12:2 • John 6:60-71

Friday: Gen. 24:1-27 • Heb. 12:3-11 • John 7:1-13

Saturday: Gen. 24:28-38, 49-51 • Heb. 12:12-29 • John 7:14-36

Fifth Sunday after the Epiphany

Set us free, O God, from the bondage of our sins, and give us the liberty of that abundant life which you have made known to us in your Son our Savior Jesus Christ; who lives and reigns with you, in the unity of the Holy Spirit, one God, now and for ever. Amen.

Sunday: Gen. 24:50-67 • 2 Tim. 2:14-21 • Mark 10:13-22

Monday: Gen. 25:19-34 • Heb. 13:1-16 • John 7:37-52

Tuesday: Gen. 26:1-6, 12-33 • Heb. 13:17-25 • John 7:53-8:11

Wednesday: Gen. 27:1-29 • Rom. 12:1-8 • John 8:12-20

Thursday: Gen. 27:30-45 • Rom. 12:9-21 • John 8:21-32

Friday: Gen. 27:46-28:4, 10-22 • Rom. 13:1-14 • John 8:33-47

Saturday: Gen. 29:1-20 • Rom. 14:1-23 • John 8:47-59

Sixth Sunday after the Epiphany
O God, the strength of all who put their trust in you: Mercifully accept our prayers; and because in our weakness we can do nothing good without you, give us the help of your grace, that in keeping your commandments we may please you both in will and deed; through Jesus Christ our Lord, who lives and reigns with you and the Holy Spirit, one God, for ever and ever. Amen.

Sunday: Gen. 29:20-35 • 1 Tim. 3:14-4:10 • Mark 10:23-31

Monday: Gen. 30:1-24 • 1 John 1:1-10 • John 9:1-17

Tuesday: Gen. 31:1-24 • 1 John 2:1-11 • John 9:18-41

Wednesday: Gen. 31:25-50 • 1 John 2:12-17 • John 10:1-18

Thursday: Gen. 32:3-21 • 1 John 2:18-29 • John 10:19-30

Friday: Gen. 32:22-33:17 • 1 John 3:1-10 • John 10:31-42

Saturday: Gen. 35:1-20 • 1 John 3:11-18 • John 11:1-16

Seventh Sunday after the Epiphany
O Lord, you have taught us that without love whatever we do is worth nothing; Send your Holy Spirit and pour into our hearts your greatest gift, which is love, the true bond of peace and of all virtue, without which whoever lives is accounted dead before you. Grant this for the sake of your only Son Jesus Christ, who lives and reigns with you and the Holy Spirit, one God, now and for ever. Amen.

Sunday: Prov. 1:20-33 • 2 Cor. 5:11-21 • Mark 10:35-45

Monday: Prov. 3:11-20 • 1 John 3:18-4:6 • John 11:17-29

Tuesday: Prov. 4:1-27 • 1 John 4:7-21 • John 11:30-44

Wednesday: Prov. 6:1-19 • 1 John 5:1-12 • John 11:45-54

Thursday: Prov. 7:1-27 • 1 John 5:13-21 • John 11:55-12:8

Friday: Prov. 8:1-21 • Philemon 1-25 • John 12:9-19

Saturday: Prov. 8:22-36 • 2 Tim. 1:1-14 • John 12:20-26

Eighth Sunday after the Epiphany

Most loving Father, whose will it is for us to give thanks for all things, to fear nothing but the loss of you, and to cast all our care on you who care for us: Preserve us from faithless fears and worldly anxieties, that no clouds of this mortal life may hide from us the light of that love which is immortal, and which you have manifested to us in your Son Jesus Christ our Lord; who lives and reigns with you, in the unity of the Holy Spirit, one God, now and for ever. Amen.

Sunday: Prov. 9:1-12 • 2 Cor. 9:6b-15 • Mark 10:46-52

Monday: Prov. 10:1-12 • 2 Tim. 1:15-2:13 • John 12:27-36a

Tuesday: Prov. 15:16-33 • 2 Tim. 2:14-26 • John 12:36b-50

Wednesday: Prov. 17:1-20 • 2 Tim. 3:1-17 • John 13:1-20

Thursday: Prov. 21:30-22:6 • 2 Tim. 4:1-8 • John 13:21-30

Friday: Prov. 23:19-21, 29-24:2 • 2 Tim. 4:9-22 • John 13:31-38

Saturday: Prov. 25:15-28 • Phil. 1:1-11 • John 18:1-14

Last Sunday after the Epiphany

O God, who before the passion of your only-begotten Son revealed his glory upon the holy mountain: Grant to us that we, beholding by faith the light of his countenance, may be strengthened to bear our cross, and be changed into his likeness from glory to glory; through Jesus Christ our Lord, who lives and reigns with you and the Holy Spirit, one God, for ever and ever. Amen.

Sunday: Prov. 26:1-12 • 2 Cor. 3:7-18 • Luke 9:18-27

Monday: Prov. 27:1-6, 10-12 • Phil. 2:1-13 • John 18:15-27

Tuesday: Prov. 30:1-4, 24-33 • Phil. 3:1-11 • John 18:28-38

Ash Wednesday

Almighty and everlasting God, you hate nothing you have made and forgive the sins of all who are penitent: Create and make in us new and contrite hearts, that we, worthily lamenting our sins and acknowledging our wretchedness, may obtain of you, the God of all mercy, perfect remission and forgiveness; through Jesus Christ our Lord, who lives and reigns with you and the Holy Spirit, one God, for ever and ever. Amen.

Ash Wednesday: Amos 5:6-15 • Heb. 12:1-14 • Luke 18:9-14

Thursday: Hab. 3:1-18 • Phil. 3:12-21 • John 17:1-8

Friday: Ezekiel 18:1-4, 25-32 • Phil. 4:1-9 • John 17:9-19

Saturday: Ezekiel 39:21-29 • Phil. 4:10-20 • John 17:20-26

First Sunday in Lent

Almighty God, whose blessed Son was led by the Spirit to be tempted by Satan; Come quickly to help us who are assaulted by many temptations; and, as you know the weaknesses of each of us, let each one find you mighty to save; through Jesus Christ your Son our Lord, who lives and reigns with you and the Holy Spirit, one God, now and for ever. Amen.

Sunday: Daniel 9:3-10 • Heb. 2:10-18 • John 12:44-50

Monday: Gen. 37:1-11 • 1 Cor. 1:1-19 • Mark 1:1-13

Tuesday: Gen. 37:12-24 • 1 Cor. 1:20-31 • Mark 1:14-28

Wednesday: Gen. 37:25-36 • 1 Cor. 2:1-13 • Mark 1:29-45

Thursday: Gen. 39:1-23 • 1 Cor. 2:14-3:15 • Mark 2:1-12

Friday: Gen. 40:1-23 • 1 Cor. 3:16-23 • Mark 2:13-22

Saturday: Gen. 41:1-13 • 1 Cor. 4:1-7 • Mark 2:23-3:6

Second Sunday in Lent

O God, whose glory it is always to have mercy: Be gracious to all who have gone astray from your ways, and bring them again with penitent hearts and steadfast faith to embrace and hold fast the unchangeable truth of your Word, Jesus Christ your Son; who with you and the Holy Spirit lives and reigns, one God, for ever and ever. Amen.

Sunday: Gen. 41:14-45 • Rom. 6:3-14 • John 5:19-24

Monday: Gen. 41:46-57 • 1 Cor. 4:8-21 • Mark 3:7-19a

Tuesday: Gen. 42:1-17 • 1 Cor. 5:1-8 • Mark 3:19b-35

Wednesday: Gen. 42:18-28 • 1 Cor. 5:9-6:8 • Mark 4:1-20

Thursday: Gen. 42:29-38 • 1 Cor. 6:12-20 • Mark 4:21-34

Friday: Gen. 43:1-15 • 1 Cor. 7:1-9 • Mark 4:35-41

Saturday: Gen. 43:16-34 • 1 Cor. 7:10-24 • Mark 5:1-20

Third Sunday in Lent
Almighty God, you know that we have no power in ourselves to help
ourselves: Keep us both outwardly in our bodies and inwardly in our
souls, that we may be defended from all adversities which may happen to
the body, and from all evil thoughts which may assault and hurt the
soul; through Jesus Christ our Lord, who lives and reigns with you and
the Holy Spirit, one God, for ever and ever. Amen.

Sunday: Gen. 44:1-17 • Rom. 8:1-10 • John 5:25-29

Monday: Gen. 44:18-34 • 1 Cor. 7:25-31 • Mark 5:21-43

Tuesday: Gen. 45:1-15 • 1 Cor. 7:32-40 • Mark 6:1-13

Wednesday: Gen. 45:16-28 • 1 Cor. 8:1-13 • Mark 6:13-29

Thursday: Gen. 46:1-7, 28-34 • 1 Cor. 9:1-15 • Mark 6:30-46

Friday: Gen. 47:1-26 • 1 Cor. 9:16-27 • Mark 6:47-56

Saturday: Gen. 47:27-48:7 • 1 Cor. 10:1-13 • Mark 7:1-23

Fourth Sunday in Lent
Gracious Father, whose blessed Son Jesus Christ came down from
heaven to be the true bread which gives life to the world: Evermore give
us this bread, that he may live in us, and we in him; who lives and
reigns with you and the Holy Spirit, one God, now and for ever. Amen.

Sunday: Gen. 48:8-22 • Rom. 8:11-25 • John 6:27-40

Monday: Gen. 49:1-28 • 1 Cor. 10:14-11:1 • Mark 7:24-37

Tuesday: Gen. 49:29-50:14 • 1 Cor. 11:17-34 • Mark 8:1-10

Wednesday: Gen. 50:15-26 • 1 Cor. 12:1-11 • Mark 8:11-26

Thursday: Exodus 1:6-22 • 1 Cor. 12:12-26 • Mark 8:27-9:1

Friday: Exodus 2:1-22 • 1 Cor. 12:27-13:3 • Mark 9:2-13

Saturday: Exodus 2:23-3:15 • 1 Cor. 13:1-13 • Mark 9:14-29

Fifth Sunday in Lent
Almighty God, you alone can bring into order the unruly wills and affections of sinners: Grant your people grace to love what you command and desire what you promise; that, among the swift and varied changes of the world, our hearts may surely there be fixed where true joys are to be found; through Jesus Christ our Lord, who lives and reigns with you and the Holy Spirit, one God, now and for ever. Amen.

Sunday: Exodus 3:16-4:12 • Rom. 12:1-21 • John 8:46-59

Monday: Exodus 4:10-31 • 1 Cor. 14:1-19 • Mark 9:30-41

Tuesday: Exodus 5:1-6:1 • 1 Cor. 14:20-33a, 39-40 • Mark 9:42-50

Wednesday: Exodus 7:8-24 • 2 Cor. 2:14-3:6 • Mark 10:1-16

Thursday: Exodus 7:25-8:19 • 2 Cor. 3:7-18 • Mark 10:17-31

Friday: Exodus 9:13-35 • 2 Cor. 4:1-12 • Mark 10:32-45

Saturday: Exodus 10:21-11:8 • 2 Cor. 4:13-18 • Mark 10:46-52

Palm Sunday
Almighty and everliving God, in your tender love for the human race you sent your Son our Savior Jesus Christ to take upon him our nature, and to suffer death upon the cross, giving us the example of his great humility: Mercifully grant that we may walk in the way of his suffering, and also share in his resurrection; through Jesus Christ our Lord, who lives and reigns with you and the Holy Spirit, one God, for ever and ever. Amen.

Palm Sunday: Zech. 12:9-11; 13:1, 7-9 • 1 Tim. 6:12-16 • Luke 19:28-48

Monday: Lam. 1:1-2, 6-12 • 2 Cor. 1:1-7 • Mark 11:12-25

Tuesday: Lam. 1:17-22 • 2 Cor. 1:8-22 • Mark 11:27-33

Wednesday: Lam. 2:1-9 • 2 Cor. 1:23-2:11 • Mark 12:1-11

Maundy Thursday: Lam. 2:10-18 • 1 Cor. 10:14-17; 11:27-32 • Mark 14:12-25

Good Friday
Almighty God, we pray you graciously to behold this your family, for whom our Lord Jesus Christ was willing to be betrayed, and given into the hands of sinners, and to suffer death upon the cross; who now lives and reigns with you and the Holy Spirit, one God, for ever and ever. Amen.

Good Friday: Lam. 3:1-9, 19-33 • 1 Peter 1:10-20 • John 19:17-30

Holy Saturday
O God, Creator of heaven and earth: Grant that, as the crucified body of your dear Son was laid in the tomb and rested on this holy Sabbath, so we may await with him the coming of the third day, and rise with him to newness of life; who now lives and reigns with you and the Holy Spirit, one God, for ever and ever. Amen.

Holy Saturday: Lam. 3:37-58 • Heb. 4:1-16 • Rom. 8:1-11

Easter Sunday
Almighty God, who through your only-begotten Son Jesus Christ overcame death and opened to us the gate of everlasting life: Grant that we, who celebrate with joy the day of the Lord's resurrection, may be raised from the death of sin by your life-giving Spirit; through Jesus

Christ our Lord, who lives and reigns with you and the Holy Spirit, one God, now and for ever. Amen.

Easter Sunday: Isaiah 51:9-11 • Rom. 6:1-11 • John 20:1-23

Monday: Exodus 12:14-27 • 1 Cor. 15:1-11 • Mark 16:1-8

Tuesday: Exodus 12:28-39 • 1 Cor. 15:12-28 • Mark 16:9-20

Wednesday: Exodus 12:40-51 • 1 Cor. 15:29-41 • Matt. 28:1-16

Thursday: Exodus 13:3-10 • 1 Cor. 15:41-50 • Matt. 28:16-20

Friday: Exodus 13:1-2, 11-16 • 1 Cor. 15:51-58 • Luke 24:1-12

Saturday: Exodus 13:17-14:4 • 2 Cor. 4:16-5:10 • Mark 12:18-27

Second Sunday of Easter
Almighty and everlasting God, who in the Paschal mystery established the new covenant of reconciliation: Grant that all who have been reborn into the fellowship of Christ's Body may show forth in their lives what they profess by their faith; through Jesus Christ our Lord, who lives and reigns with you and the Holy Spirit, one God, for ever and ever. Amen.

Sunday: Exodus 14:5-22 • 1 John 1:1-7 • John 14:1-7

Monday: Exodus 14:21-31 • 1 Peter 1:1-12 • John 14:1-17

Tuesday: Exodus 15:1-21 • 1 Peter 1:13-25 • John 14:18-31

Wednesday: Exodus 15:22-16:10 • 1 Peter 2:1-10 • John 15:1-11

Thursday: Exodus 16:10-21 • 1 Peter 2:11-25 • John 15:12-27

Friday: Exodus 16:22-36 • 1 Peter 3:13-4:6 • John 16:1-15

Saturday: Exodus 17:1-16 • 1 Peter 4:7-19 • John 16:16-33

Third Sunday of Easter
O God, whose blessed Son made himself known to his disciples in the breaking of bread: Open the eyes of our faith, that we may behold him in all his redeeming work; who lives and reigns with you, in the unity of the Holy Spirit, one God, now and for ever. Amen.

Sunday: Exodus 18:1-12 • 1 John 2:7-17 • Mark 16:9-20

Monday: Exodus 18:13-27 • 1 Peter 5:1-14 • Matt. 1:1-17, 3:1-6

Tuesday: Exodus 19:1-16 • Col. 1:1-14 • Matt. 3:7-12

Wednesday: Exodus 19:16-25 • Col. 1:15-23 • Matt. 3:13-17

Thursday: Exodus 20:1-21 • Col. 1:24-2:7 • Matt. 4:1-11

Friday: Exodus 24:1-18 • Col. 2:8-23 • Matt. 4:12-17

Saturday: Exodus 25:1-22 • Col. 3:1-17 • Matt. 4:18-25

Fourth Sunday of Easter
O God, whose Son Jesus is the good shepherd of your people; Grant that when we hear his voice we may know him who calls us each by name, and follow where he leads; who, with you and the Holy Spirit, lives and reigns, one God, for ever and ever. Amen.

Sunday: Exodus 25:1-4, 30-38 • 1 John 2:18-29 • Mark 6:30-44

Monday: Exodus 32:1-20 • Col. 3:18-4:18 • Matt. 5:1-10

Tuesday: Exodus 32:21-34 • 1 Thess. 1:1-10 • Matt. 5:11-16

Wednesday: Exodus 33:1-23 • 1 Thess. 2:1-12 • Matt. 5:17-20

Thursday: Exodus 34:1-17 • 1 Thess. 2:13-20 • Matt. 5:21-26

Friday: Exodus 34:18-35 • 1 Thess. 3:1-13 • Matt. 5:27-37

Saturday: Exodus 40:18-38 • 1 Thess. 4:1-12 • Matt. 5:38-48

Fifth Sunday of Easter

Almighty God, whom truly to know is everlasting life: Grant us so perfectly to know your Son Jesus Christ to be the way, the truth, and the life, that we may steadfastly follow his steps in the way that leads to eternal life; through Jesus Christ your Son our Lord, who lives and reigns with you, in the unity of the Holy Spirit, one God, for ever and ever. Amen.

Sunday: Lev. 8:1-13, 30-36 • Heb. 12:1-14 • Luke 4:16-30

Monday: Lev. 16:1-19 • 1 Thess. 4:13-18 • Matt. 6:1-6, 16-18

Tuesday: Lev. 16:20-34 • 1 Thess. 5:1-11 • Matt. 6:7-15

Wednesday: Lev. 19:1-18 • 1 Thess. 5:12-28 • Matt. 6:19-24

Thursday: Lev. 19:26-37 • 2 Thess. 1:1-12 • Matt. 6:25-34

Friday: Lev. 23:1-22 • 2 Thess. 2:1-17 • Matt. 7:1-12

Saturday: Lev. 23:23-44 • 2 Thess. 3:1-18 • Matt. 7:13-21

Sixth Sunday of Easter

O God, you have prepared for those who love you such good things as surpass our understanding: Pour into our hearts such love towards you, that we, loving you in all things and above all things, may obtain your promises, which exceed all that we can desire; through Jesus Christ our Lord, who lives and reigns with you and the Holy Spirit, one God, for ever and ever. Amen.

Sunday: Lev. 25:1-17 • James 1:2-8, 16-18 • Luke 12:13-21

Monday: Lev. 25:35-55 • Col. 1:9-14 • Matt. 13:1-16

Tuesday: Lev. 26:1-20 • 1 Tim. 2:1-6 • Matt. 13:18-23

Wednesday: Lev. 26:27-42 • Eph. 1:1-10 • Matt. 22:41-46

Ascension Day: Daniel 7:9-14 • Heb. 2:5-18 • Matt. 28:16-20

Friday: 1 Sam. 2:1-10 • Eph. 2:1-10 • Matt. 7:22-27

Saturday: Num.11:16-17, 24-29 • Eph. 2:11-22 • Matt. 7:28-8:4

Seventh Sunday of Easter
*O God, the King of glory, you have exalted your only Son Jesus Christ
with great triumph to your kingdom in heaven: Do not leave us
comfortless, but send us your Holy Spirit to strengthen us, and exalt us
to that place where our Savior Christ has gone before; who lives and
reigns with you and the Holy Spirit, one God, in glory everlasting.
Amen.*

Sunday: Exodus 3:1-12 • Heb. 12:18-29 • Luke 10:17-24

Monday: Joshua 1:1-9 • Eph. 3:1-13 • Matt. 8:5-17

Tuesday: 1 Sam. 16:1-13a • Eph. 3:14-21 • Matt. 8:18-27

Wednesday: Isaiah 4:2-6 • Eph. 4:1-16 • Matt. 8:28-34

Thursday: Zech. 4:1-14 • Eph. 4:17-32 • Matt. 9:1-8

Friday: Jer. 31:27-34 • Eph. 5:1-20 • Matt. 9:9-17

Saturday: Ezekiel 36:22-27 • Eph. 6:10-24 • Matt. 9:18-26

Pentecost Sunday
*Almighty God, on this day you opened the way of eternal life to every
race and nation by the promised gift of your Holy Spirit: Shed abroad*

this gift throughout the world by the preaching of the Gospel, that it may reach to the ends of the earth; through Jesus Christ our Lord, who lives and reigns with you, in the unity of the Holy Spirit, one God, for ever and ever. Amen.

Pentecost Sunday: Deut. 16:9-12 • Acts 4:18-21, 23-33 • John 4:19-26

On the weekdays which follow, the readings are taken from the numbered Proper (one through six) which corresponds most closely to the date of Pentecost.

Ordinary Time

Proper 1
Week of the Sunday closest to May 11

Remember, O Lord, what you have wrought in us and not what we deserve; and, as you have called us to your service, make us worthy of our calling; through Jesus Christ our Lord, who lives and reigns with you and the Holy Spirit, one God, now and for ever. Amen.

Monday: Ezekiel 33:1-11 • 1 John 1:1-10 • Matt. 9:27-34

Tuesday: Ezekiel 33:21-33 • 1 John 2:1-11 • Matt. 9:35-10:4

Wednesday: Ezekiel 34:1-16 • 1 John 2:12-17 • Matt. 10:5-14

Thursday: Ezekiel 37:21b-28 • 1 John 2:18-29 • Matt. 10:16-23

Friday: Ezekiel 39:21-29 • 1 John 3:1-10 • Matt. 10:24-33

Saturday: Ezekiel 47:1-12 • 1 John 3:11-18 • Matt. 10:34-42

Proper 2
Week of the Sunday closest to May 18

Almighty and merciful God, in your goodness keep us, we pray, from all things that may hurt us, that we, being ready both in mind and body, may accomplish with free hearts those things which belong to your purpose; through Jesus Christ our Lord, who lives and reigns with you and the Holy Spirit, one God, now and for ever. Amen.

Monday: Prov. 3:11-20 • 1 John 3:18-4:6 • Matt. 11:1-6

Tuesday: Prov. 4:1-27 • 1 John 4:7-21 • Matt. 11:7-15

Wednesday: Prov. 6:1-19 • 1 John 5:1-12 • Matt. 11:16-24

Thursday: Prov. 7:1-27 • 1 John 5:13-21 • Matt. 11:25-30

Friday: Prov. 8:1-21 • 2 John 1-13 • Matt. 12:1-14

Saturday: Prov. 8:22-36 • 3 John 1-15 • Matt. 12:15-21

Proper 3
Week of the Sunday closest to May 25

Grant, O Lord, that the course of this world may be peaceably governed by your providence; and that your Church may joyfully serve you in confidence and serenity; through Jesus Christ our Lord, who lives and reigns with you and the Holy Spirit, one God, for ever and ever. Amen.

Sunday: Prov. 9:1-12 • Acts 8:14-25 • Luke 10:25-28, 38-42

Monday: Prov. 10:1-12 • 1 Tim. 1:1-17 • Matt. 12:22-32

Tuesday: Prov. 15:16-33 • 1 Tim. 1:18-2:8 • Matt. 12:33-42

Wednesday: Prov. 17:1-20 • 1 Tim. 3:1-16 • Matt. 12:43-50

Thursday: Prov. 21:30-22:6 • 1 Tim. 4:1-16 • Matt. 13:24-30

Friday: Prov. 23:19-21, 29-24:2 • 1 Tim. 5:17-25 • Matt. 13:31-35

Saturday: Prov. 25:15-28 • 1 Tim. 6:6-21 • Matt. 13:36-43

Proper 4
Week of the Sunday closest to June 1

O God, your never-failing providence sets in order all things both in heaven and earth: Put away from us, we entreat you, all hurtful things, and give us those things which are profitable for us; through Jesus Christ our Lord, who lives and reigns with you and the Holy Spirit, one God, for ever and ever. Amen.

Sunday: Ecc. 1:1-11 • Acts 8:26-40 • Luke 11:1-13

Monday: Ecc. 2:1-15 • Galatians 1:1-17 • Matt. 13:44-52

Tuesday: Ecc. 2:16-26 • Galatians 1:18-2:10 • Matt. 13:53-58

Wednesday: Ecc. 3:1-15 • Galatians 2:11-21 • Matt. 14:1-12

Thursday: Ecc. 3:16-4:3 • Galatians 3:1-14 • Matt. 14:13-21

Friday: Ecc. 5:1-7 • Galatians 3:15-22 • Matt. 14:22-36

Saturday: Ecc. 5:8-20 • Galatians 3:23-4:11 • Matt. 15:1-20

Proper 5
Week of the Sunday closest to June 8

O God, from whom all good proceeds: Grant that by your inspiration we may think those things that are right, and by your merciful guiding may do them; through Jesus Christ our Lord, who lives and reigns with you and the Holy Spirit, one God, for ever and ever. Amen.

Sunday: Ecc. 6:1-12 • Acts 10:9-23 • Luke 12:32-40

Monday: Ecc. 7:1-14 • Galatians 4:12-20 • Matt. 15:21-28

Tuesday: Ecc. 8:14-9:10 • Galatians 4:21-31 • Matt. 15:29-39

Wednesday: Ecc. 9:11-18 • Galatians 5:1-15 • Matt. 16:1-12

Thursday: Ecc. 11:1-8 • Galatians 5:16-24 • Matt. 16:13-20

Friday: Ecc. 11:9-12:14 • Galatians 5:25-6:10 • Matt. 16:21-28

Saturday: Num. 3:1-13 • Galatians 6:11-18 • Matt. 17:1-13

Proper 6
Week of the Sunday closest to June 15

*Keep, O Lord, your household the Church in your steadfast faith and
love, that through your grace we may proclaim your truth with
boldness, and minister your justice with compassion; for the sake of our
Savior Jesus Christ, who lives and reigns with you and the Holy Spirit,
one God, now and for ever. Amen.*

Sunday: Num. 6:22-27 • Acts 13:1-12 • Luke 12:41-48

Monday: Num. 9:15-23; 10:29-36 • Rom. 1:1-15 • Matt. 17:14-21

Tuesday: Num. 11:1-23 • Rom. 1:16-25 • Matt. 17:22-27

Wednesday: Num. 11:24-35 • Rom. 1:28-2:11 • Matt. 18:1-9

Thursday: Num. 12:1-16 • Rom. 2:12-24 • Matt. 18:10-20

Friday: Num. 13:1-3, 21-30 • Rom. 2:25-3:8 • Matt. 18:21-35

Saturday: Num. 13:31-14:25 • Rom. 3:9-20 • Matt. 19:1-12

Proper 7
Week of the Sunday closest to June 22

O Lord, make us have perpetual love and reverence for your holy Name, for you never fail to help and govern those whom you have set upon the sure foundation of your loving-kindness; through Jesus Christ our Lord, who lives and reigns with you and the Holy Spirit, one God, for ever and ever. Amen.

Sunday: Num. 14:26-45 • Acts 15:1-12 • Luke 12:49-56

Monday: Num. 16:1-19 • Rom. 3:21-31 • Matt. 19:13-22

Tuesday: Num. 16:20-35 • Rom. 4:1-12 • Matt. 19:23-30

Wednesday: Num. 16:36-50 • Rom. 4:13-25 • Matt. 20:1-16

Thursday: Num. 17:1-11 • Rom. 5:1-11 • Matt. 20:17-28

Friday: Num. 20:1-13 • Rom. 5:12-21 • Matt. 20:29-34

Saturday: Num. 20:14-29 • Rom. 6:1-11 • Matt. 21:1-11

Proper 8
Week of the Sunday closest to June 29

Almighty God, you have built your Church upon the foundation of the apostles and prophets, Jesus Christ himself being the chief cornerstone: Grant us so to be joined together in unity of spirit by their teaching, that we may be made a holy temple acceptable to you; through Jesus Christ our Lord, who lives and reigns with you and the Holy Spirit, one God, for ever and ever. Amen.

Sunday: Num. 21:4-9, 21-35 • Acts 17:12-34 • Luke 13:10-17

Monday: Num. 22:1-21 • Rom. 6:12-23 • Matt. 21:12-22

Tuesday: Num. 22:21-38 • Rom. 7:1-12 • Matt. 21:23-32

Wednesday: Num. 22:41-23:12 • Rom. 7:13-25 • Matt. 21:33-46

Thursday: Num. 23:11-26 • Rom. 8:1-11 • Matt. 22:1-14

Friday: Num. 24:1-13 • Rom. 8:12-17 • Matt. 22:15-22

Saturday: Num. 24:12-25 • Rom. 8:18-25 • Matt. 22:23-40

Proper 9
Week of the Sunday closest to July 6

O God, you have taught us to keep all your commandments by loving you and our neighbor: Grant us the grace of your Holy Spirit, that we may be devoted to you with our whole heart, and united to one another with pure affection; through Jesus Christ our Lord, who lives and reigns with you and the Holy Spirit, one God, for ever and ever. Amen.

Sunday: Num. 27:12-23 • Acts 19:11-20 • Mark 1:14-20

Monday: Num. 32:1-6, 16-27 • Rom. 8:26-30 • Matt. 23:1-12

Tuesday: Num. 35:1-3, 9-34 • Rom. 8:31-39 • Matt. 23:13-26

Wednesday: Deut. 1:1-18 • Rom. 9:1-18 • Matt. 23:27-39

Thursday: Deut. 3:18-28 • Rom. 9:19-33 • Matt. 24:1-14

Friday: Deut. 31:7-13, 24-32:4 • Rom. 10:1-13 • Matt. 24:15-31

Saturday: Deut. 34:1-12 • Rom. 10:14-21 • Matt. 24:32-51

Proper 10
Week of the Sunday closest to July 13

O Lord, mercifully receive the prayers of your people who call upon you, and grant that they may know and understand what things they ought to do, and also may have grace and power faithfully to accomplish them; through Jesus Christ our Lord, who lives and reigns with you and the Holy Spirit, one God, now and for ever. Amen.

Sunday: Joshua 1:1-18 • Acts 21:3-15 • Mark 1:21-27

Monday: Joshua 2:1-14 • Rom. 11:1-12 • Matt. 25:1-13

Tuesday: Joshua 2:15-24 • Rom. 11:13-24 • Matt. 25:14-30

Wednesday: Joshua 3:1-13 • Rom. 11:25-36 • Matt. 25:31-46

Thursday: Joshua 3:14-4:7 • Rom. 12:1-8 • Matt. 26:1-16

Friday: Joshua 4:19-5:1, 10-15 • Rom. 12:9-21 • Matt. 26:17-25

Saturday: Joshua 6:1-14 • Rom. 13:1-7 • Matt. 26:26-35

Proper 11
Week of the Sunday closest to July 20

Almighty God, the fountain of all wisdom, you know our necessities before we ask and our ignorance in asking: Have compassion on our weakness, and mercifully give us those things which for our unworthiness we dare not, and for our blindness we cannot ask; through the worthiness of your Son Jesus Christ our Lord, who lives and reigns with you and the Holy Spirit, one God, now and for ever. Amen.

Sunday: Joshua 6:15-27 • Acts 22:30-23:11 • Mark 2:1-12

Monday: Joshua 7:1-13 • Rom. 13:8-14 • Matt. 26:36-46

Tuesday: Joshua 8:1-22 • Rom. 14:1-12 • Matt. 26:47-56

Wednesday: Joshua 8:30-35 • Rom. 14:13-23 • Matt. 26:57-68

Thursday: Joshua 9:3-21 • Rom. 15:1-13 • Matt. 26:69-75

Friday: Joshua 9:22-10:15 • Rom. 15:14-24 • Matt. 27:1-10

Saturday: Joshua 23:1-16 • Rom. 15:25-33 • Matt. 27:11-23

Proper 12
Week of the Sunday closest to July 27

O God, the protector of all who trust in you, without whom nothing is strong, nothing is holy: Increase and multiply upon us your mercy; that, with you as our ruler and guide, we may so pass through things temporal, that we lose not the things eternal; through Jesus Christ our Lord, who lives and reigns with you and the Holy Spirit, one God, for ever and ever. Amen.

Sunday: Joshua 24:1-15 • Acts 28:23-31 • Mark 2:23-28

Monday: Joshua 24:16-33 • Rom. 16:1-16 • Matt. 27:24-31

Tuesday: Judges 2:1-5, 11-23 • Rom. 16:17-27 • Matt. 27:32-44

Wednesday: Judges 3:12-30 • Acts 1:1-14 • Matt. 27:45-54

Thursday: Judges 4:4-23 • Acts 1:15-26 • Matt. 27:55-66

Friday: Judges 5:1-18 • Acts 2:1-21 • Matt. 28:1-10

Saturday: Judges 5:19-31 • Acts 2:22-36 • Matt. 28:11-20

Proper 13

Week of the Sunday closest to August 3

Let your continual mercy, O Lord, cleanse and defend your Church; and, because it cannot continue in safety without your help, protect and govern it always by your goodness; through Jesus Christ our Lord, who lives and reigns with you and the Holy Spirit, one God, for ever and ever. Amen.

Sunday: Judges 6:1-24 • 2 Cor. 9:6-15 • Mark 3:20-30

Monday: Judges 6:25-40 • Acts 2:37-47 • John 1:1-18

Tuesday: Judges 7:1-18 • Acts 3:1-11 • John 1:19-28

Wednesday: Judges 7:19-8:12 • Acts 3:12-26 • John 1:29-42

Thursday: Judges 8:22-35 • Acts 4:1-12 • John 1:43-51

Friday: Judges 9:1-16, 19-21 • Acts 4:13-31 • John 2:1-12

Saturday: Judges 9:22-25, 50-57 • Acts 4:32-5:11 • John 2:13-25

Proper 14

Week of the Sunday closest to August 10

Grant to us, Lord, we pray, the spirit to think and do always those things that are right, that we, who cannot exist without you, may by you be enabled to live according to your will; through Jesus Christ our Lord, who lives and reigns with you and the Holy Spirit, one God, for ever and ever. Amen.

Sunday: Judges 11:1-40 • 2 Cor. 11:21b-31 • Mark 4:35-41

Monday: Judges 12:1-7 • Acts 5:12-26 • John 3:1-21

Tuesday: Judges 13:1-15 • Acts 5:27-42 • John 3:22-36

Wednesday: Judges 13:15-24 • Acts 6:1-15 • John 4:1-26

Thursday: Judges 14:1-19 • Acts 6:15-7:16 • John 4:27-42

Friday: Judges 14:20-15:20 • Acts 7:17-29 • John 4:43-54

Saturday: Judges 16:1-14 • Acts 7:30-43 • John 5:1-18

Proper 15
Week of the Sunday closest to August 17

Almighty God, you have given your only Son to be for us a sacrifice for sin, and also an example of godly life: Give us grace to receive thankfully the fruits of this redeeming work, and to follow daily in the blessed steps of his most holy life; through Jesus Christ your Son our Lord, who lives and reigns with you and the Holy Spirit, one God, now and for ever. Amen.

Sunday: Judges 16:15-31 • 2 Cor. 13:1-11 • Mark 5:25-34

Monday: Judges 17:1-13 • Acts 7:44-8:1a • John 5:19-29

Tuesday: Judges 18:1-15 • Acts 8:1-13 • John 5:30-47

Wednesday: Judges 18:16-31 • Acts 8:14-25 • John 6:1-15

Thursday: Job 1:1-22 • Acts 8:26-40 • John 6:16-27

Friday: Job 2:1-13 • Acts 9:1-9 • John 6:27-40

Saturday: Job 3:1-26 • Acts 9:10-19a • John 6:41-51

Proper 16

Week of the Sunday closest to August 24

Grant, O merciful God, that your Church, being gathered together in unity by your Holy Spirit, may show forth your power among all peoples, to the glory of your Name; through Jesus Christ our Lord, who lives and reigns with you and the Holy Spirit, one God, for ever and ever. Amen.

Sunday: Job 4:1-6, 12-21 • Rev. 4:1-11 • Mark 6:1-6a

Monday: Job 4:1; 5:1-27 • Acts 9:19b-31 • John 6:52-59

Tuesday: Job 6:1-4, 8-15, 21 • Acts 9:32-43 • John 6:60-71

Wednesday: Job 6:1; 7:1-21 • Acts 10:1-16 • John 7:1-13

Thursday: Job 8:1-10, 20-22 • Acts 10:17-33 • John 7:14-36

Friday: Job 9:1-15, 32-35 • Acts 10:34-48 • John 7:37-52

Saturday: Job 9:1; 10:1-9, 16-22 • Acts 11:1-18 • John 8:12-20

Proper 17

Week of the Sunday closest to August 31

Lord of all power and might, the author and giver of all good things: Graft in our hearts the love of your Name; increase in us true religion; nourish us with all goodness; and bring forth in us the fruit of good works; through Jesus Christ our Lord, who lives and reigns with you and the Holy Spirit, one God, for ever and ever. Amen.

Sunday: Job 11:1-9, 13-20 • Rev. 5:1-14 • Matt. 5:1-12

Monday: Job 12:1-6, 13-25 • Acts 11:19-30 • John 8:21-32

Tuesday: Job 12:1; 13:3-17, 21-27 • Acts 12:1-17 • John 8:33-47

Wednesday: Job 12:1; 14:1-22 • Acts 12:18-25 • John 8:47-59

Thursday: Job 16:16-22; 17:1, 13-16 • Acts 13:1-12 • John 9:1-17

Friday: Job 19:1-7, 14-27 • Acts 13:13-25 • John 9:18-41

Saturday: Job 22:1-4, 21-23:7 • Acts 13:26-43 • John 10:1-18

Proper 18
Week of the Sunday closest to September 7

Grant us, O Lord, to trust in you with all our hearts; for, as you always resist the proud who confide in their own strength, so you never forsake those who make their boast of your mercy; through Jesus Christ our Lord, who lives and reigns with you and the Holy Spirit, one God, now and for ever. Amen.

Sunday: Job 25:1-6; 27:1-6 • Rev. 14:1-7, 13 • Matt. 5:13-20

Monday: Job 32:1-19, 33:1, 19-28 • Acts 13:44-52 • John 10:19-30

Tuesday: Job 29:1-20 • Acts 14:1-18 • John 10:31-42

Wednesday: Job 29:1; 30:1-31 • Acts 14:19-28 • John 11:1-16

Thursday: Job 29:1; 31:1-23 • Acts 15:1-11 • John 11:17-29

Friday: Job 29:1; 31:24-40 • Acts 15:12-21 • John 11:30-44

Saturday: Job 38:1-17 • Acts 15:22-35 • John 11:45-54

Proper 19

Week of the Sunday closest to September 14

O God, because without you we are not able to please you, mercifully grant that your Holy Spirit may in all things direct and rule our hearts; through Jesus Christ our Lord, who lives and reigns with you and the Holy Spirit, one God, now and for ever. Amen.

Sunday: Job 38:1, 18-41 • Rev. 18:1-8 • Matt. 5:21-26

Monday: Job 40:1-24 • Acts 15:36-16:5 • John 11:55-12:8

Tuesday: Job 40:1; 41:1-11 • Acts 16:6-15 • John 12:9-19

Wednesday: Job 42:1-17 • Acts 16:16-24 • John 12:20-26

Thursday: Job 28:1-28 • Acts 16:25-40 • John 12:27-36a

Friday: Esther 1:1-4, 10-19 • Acts 17:1-15 • John 12:36b-43

Saturday: Esther 2:5-8, 15-23 • Acts 17:16-34 • John 12:44-50

Proper 20

Week of the Sunday closest to September 21

Grant us, Lord, not to be anxious about earthly things, but to love things heavenly; and even now, while we are placed among things that are passing away, to hold fast to those that shall endure; through Jesus Christ our Lord, who lives and reigns with you and the Holy Spirit, one God, for ever and ever. Amen.

Sunday: Esther 3:1-4:3 • James 1:19-27 • Matt. 6:1-6, 16-18

Monday: Esther 4:4-17 • Acts 18:1-11 • Luke 3:1-14

Tuesday: Esther 5:1-14 • Acts 18:12-28 • Luke 3:15-22

Wednesday: Esther 6:1-14 • Acts 19:1-10 • Luke 4:1-13

Thursday: Esther 7:1-10 • Acts 19:11-20 • Luke 4:14-30

Friday: Esther 8:1-8, 15-17 • Acts 19:21-41 • Luke 4:31-37

Saturday: Hosea 1:1-2:1 • Acts 20:1-16 • Luke 4:38-44

Proper 21
Week of the Sunday closest to September 28

O God, you declare your almighty power chiefly in showing mercy and pity: Grant us the fullness of your grace, that we, running to obtain your promises, may become partakers of your heavenly treasure; through Jesus Christ our Lord, who lives and reigns with you and the Holy Spirit, one God, for ever and ever. Amen.

Sunday: Hosea 2:2-14 • James 3:1-13 • Matt. 13:44-52

Monday: Hosea 2:14-23 • Acts 20:17-38 • Luke 5:1-11

Tuesday: Hosea 4:1-10 • Acts 21:1-14 • Luke 5:12-26

Wednesday: Hosea 4:11-19 • Acts 21:15-26 • Luke 5:27-39

Thursday: Hosea 5:8-6:6 • Acts 21:27-36 • Luke 6:1-11

Friday: Hosea 10:1-15 • Acts 21:37-22:16 • Luke 6:12-26

Saturday: Hosea 11:1-9 • Acts 22:17-29 • Luke 6:27-38

Proper 22
Week of the Sunday closest to October 5

Almighty and everlasting God, you are always more ready to hear than we to pray, and to give more than we either desire or deserve: Pour upon us the abundance of your mercy, forgiving us those things of which our conscience is afraid, and giving us those good things for which we are not worthy to ask, except through the merits and mediation of Jesus Christ our Savior; who lives and reigns with you and the Holy Spirit, one God, for ever and ever. Amen.

Sunday: Hosea 13:4-14 • 1 Cor. 2:6-16 • Matt. 14:1-12

Monday: Hosea 14:1-9 • Acts 22:30-23:11 • Luke 6:39-49

Tuesday: Micah 1:1-9 • Acts 23:12-24 • Luke 7:1-17

Wednesday: Micah 2:1-13 • Acts 23:23-35 • Luke 7:18-35

Thursday: Micah 3:1-8 • Acts 24:1-23 • Luke 7:36-50

Friday: Micah 3:9-4:5 • Acts 24:24-25:12 • Luke 8:1-15

Saturday: Micah 5:1-4, 10-15 • Acts 25:13-27 • Luke 8:16-25

Proper 23
Week of the Sunday closest to October 12

Lord, we pray that your grace may always precede and follow us, that we may continually be given to good works; through Jesus Christ our Lord, who lives and reigns with you and the Holy Spirit, one God, now and for ever. Amen.

Sunday: Micah 6:1-8 • 1 Cor. 4:9-16 • Matt. 15:21-28

Monday: Micah 7:1-7 • Acts 26:1-23 • Luke 8:26-39

Tuesday: Jonah 1:1-17a • Acts 26:24-27:8 • Luke 8:40-56

Wednesday: Jonah 1:17-2:10 • Acts 27:9-26 • Luke 9:1-17

Thursday: Jonah 3:1-4:11 • Acts 27:27-44 • Luke 9:18-27

Friday: Zephaniah 1:1-9 • Acts 28:1-16 • Luke 9:28-36

Saturday: Zephaniah 1:10-18 • Acts 28:17-31 • Luke 9:37-50

Proper 24
Week of the Sunday closest to October 19

Almighty and everlasting God, in Christ you have revealed your glory among the nations: Preserve the works of your mercy, that your Church throughout the world may persevere with steadfast faith in the confession of your Name; through Jesus Christ our Lord, who lives and reigns with you and the Holy Spirit, one God, for ever and ever. Amen.

Sunday: Zephaniah 2:1-7• 1 Cor. 10:1-13 • Matt. 16:13-20

Monday: Zephaniah 2:8-15 • Rev. 7:1-8 • Luke 9:51-62

Tuesday: Nahum 2:1-13 • Rev. 7:9-17 • Luke 10:1-16

Wednesday: Nahum 2:1-13 • Rev. 8:1-13 • Luke 10:17-24

Thursday: Nahum 3:1-9 • Rev. 9:1-12 • Luke 10:25-37

Friday: Nahum 3:10-19 • Rev. 9:13-21 • Luke 10:38-42

Saturday: Leviticus 9:1-14 • Rev. 10:1-11 • Luke 11:1-13

Proper 25
Week of the Sunday closest to October 26

Almighty and everlasting God, increase in us the gifts of faith, hope, and charity; and, that we may obtain what you promise, make us love what you command; through Jesus Christ our Lord, who lives and reigns with you and the Holy Spirit, one God, for ever and ever. Amen.

Sunday: Leviticus 9:15-24 • 1 Cor. 10:15-24 • Matt. 18:15-20

Monday: Leviticus 17:1-9 • Rev. 11:1-14 • Luke 11:14-26

Tuesday: Proverbs 26:13-38 • Rev. 11:14-19 • Luke 11:27-36

Wednesday: Proverbs 27:13-27 • Rev. 12:1-6 • Luke 11:37-52

Thursday: Proverbs 28:1-13 • Rev. 12:7-17 • Luke 11:53-12:12

Friday: Proverbs 28:14-28 • Rev. 13:1-10 • Luke 12:13-31

Saturday: Proverbs 29:1-13 • Rev. 13:11-18 • Luke 12:32-48

Proper 26
Week of the Sunday closest to November 2

*Almighty and merciful God, it is only by your gift that your faithful
people offer you true and laudable service: Grant that we may run
without stumbling to obtain your heavenly promises; through Jesus
Christ our Lord, who lives and reigns with you and the Holy Spirit, one
God, now and for ever. Amen.*

Sunday: Song of Sol. 1:1-17 • 1 Cor. 12:27-13:13 • Matt. 18:21-35

Monday: Song of Sol. 2:1-17 • Rev. 14:1-13 • Luke 12:49-59

Tuesday: Song of Sol. 3:1-11 • Rev. 14:14-15:8 • Luke 13:1-9

Wednesday: Song of Sol. 4:1-16 • Rev. 16:1-11 • Luke 13:10-17

Thursday: Song of Sol. 5:1-16 • Rev. 16:12-21 • Luke 13:18-30

Friday: Song of Sol. 6:1-13 • Rev. 17:1-18 • Luke 13:31-35

Saturday: Song of Sol. 7:1-13 • Rev. 18:1-14 • Luke 14:1-11

Proper 27

Week of the Sunday closest to November 9

O God, whose blessed Son came into the world that he might destroy the works of the devil and make us children of God and heirs of eternal life: Grant that, having this hope, we may purify ourselves as he is pure; that, when he comes again with power and great glory, we may be made like him in his eternal and glorious kingdom; where he lives and reigns with you and the Holy Spirit, one God, for ever and ever. Amen.

Sunday: Song of Sol. 8:1-14 • 1 Cor. 14:1-12 • Matt. 20:1-16

Monday: Joel 1:1-13 • Rev. 18:15-24 • Luke 14:12-24

Tuesday: Joel 1:15-2:11 • Rev. 19:1-10 • Luke 14:25-35

Wednesday: Joel 2:12-19 • Rev. 19:11-21 • Luke 15:1-10

Thursday: Joel 2:21-27 • James 1:1-15 • Luke 15:1-2, 11-32

Friday: Joel 2:28-3:8 • James 1:16-27 • Luke 16:1-9

Saturday: Joel 3:9-17 • James 2:1-13 • Luke 16:10-18

Proper 28

Week of the Sunday closest to November 16

Blessed Lord, who caused all holy Scriptures to be written for our learning: Grant us so to hear them, read, mark, learn, and inwardly digest them, that we may embrace and ever hold fast the blessed hope of everlasting life, which you have given us in our Savior Jesus Christ; who lives and reigns with you and the Holy Spirit, one God, for ever and ever. Amen.

Sunday: Hab. 1:1-2:1 • Phil. 3:13-4:1 • Matt. 23:13-24

Monday: Hab. 2:1-4, 9-20 • James 2:14-26 • Luke 16:19-31

Tuesday: Hab. 3:1-18 • James 3:1-12 • Luke 17:1-10

Wednesday: Mal. 1:1, 6-14 • James 3:13-4:12 • Luke 17:11-19

Thursday: Mal. 2:1-16 • James 4:13-5:6 • Luke 17:20-37

Friday: Mal. 3:1-12 • James 5:7-12 • Luke 18:1-8

Saturday: Mal. 3:13-4:6 • James 5:13-20 • Luke 18:9-14

Proper 29
Week of the Sunday closest to November 23

Almighty and everlasting God, whose will it is to restore all things in your well-beloved Son, the King of kings and Lord of lords: Mercifully grant that the peoples of the earth, divided and enslaved by sin, may be freed and brought together under his most gracious rule; who lives and reigns with you and the Holy Spirit, one God, now and for ever. Amen.

Christ the King Sunday: Zech. 9:9-16 • 1 Peter 3:13-22 • Matt. 21:1-13

Monday: Zech. 10:1-12 • Galatians 6:1-10 • Luke 18:15-30

Tuesday: Zech. 11:4-17 • 1 Cor. 3:10-23 • Luke 18:31-43

Wednesday: Zech. 12:1-10 • Eph. 1:3-14 • Luke 19:1-10

Thursday: Zech. 13:1-9 • Eph. 1:15-23 • Luke 19:11-27

Friday: Zech. 14:1-11 • Rom. 15:7-13 • Luke 19:28-40

Saturday: Zech. 14:12-21 • Phil. 2:1-11 • Luke 19:41-48

ABOUT THE AUTHOR

Derek Vreeland is the Discipleship Pastor at Word of Life Church in St. Joseph, Missouri, where he is known for his thoughtful, humorous, and authentic teaching style. He is a graduate of Asbury Theological Seminary (D.Min.), Oral Roberts University (M.Div.), and Missouri Western State University (B.A.).

He self-identifies as a "Bible nerd," who is dedicated to reading, studying, and teaching the Bible in a way that causes people to love and follow Jesus. He has used the Daily Office Lectionary for his personal Bible reading for years.

In addition to teaching and leading discipleship ministries at Word of Life Church, Derek enjoys reading, running, and hiking. He and his wife Jenni have three sons, Wesley, Taylor, and Dylan, one daughter-in-law, Maggie, and one grandson, Leo.

He is the author of two discipleship books: *Centering Jesus: How the Lamb of God Transforms Our Communities, Ethics, and Spiritual Lives* (NavPress 2023) and *By the Way: Getting Serious About Following Jesus* (Herald Press 2019). He also wrote two reader's guides for to N.T. Wright books: *N.T. Wright and the Revolutionary Cross: A Reader's Guide to The Day the Revolution Began* (Doctrina Press 2017) and *Through the Eyes of N.T. Wright: A Reader's Guide to Paul and the Faithfulness of God* (Doctrina Press 2015).

Follow Derek on social media at @DerekVreeland. Contact him by email at derekvreeland@gmail.com.

Made in United States
Orlando, FL
23 December 2024

56473791R00055